KV-675-510

Dedication

To François de B. Gordeau, Jean Cuco and all
fly-tyers

S.-J.V.

Acknowledgments

To Jacques Authier for his encouragement, his time and his skill in fly-tying.

To Jocelyn Blais for his skill and artistry in capturing so much detail on film.

To Patsy, my wife, for her patience, understanding and secretarial help.

To Arlette Dubois for typing the original manuscript.

The Artificial Fly

A STEP-BY-STEP PICTURE GUIDE

Text by Serge-J. Vincent
Photographs by Jocelyn Blais

Adam and Charles Black · London

D1685467

First published in this edition 1979
by A & C Black (Publishers) Ltd
35 Bedford Row, London WC1R 4JH

ISBN 0 7136 1941 4

© 1979 A & C Black (Publishers) Ltd

Originally published in Canada as *La Mouche*
© 1977 Librairie Beauchemin Limitée

All rights reserved. No part of this publication may be
reproduced, stored in a retrieval system, or transmitted
in any form or by any means, electronic, mechanical,
photocopying, recording or otherwise, without prior
permission of A & C Black (Publishers) Ltd.

Vincent, Serge
    The artificial fly
    1. Fly tying
    I. Title   II. Blais, Jocelyn
    688.7′9   SH451

    ISBN 0-7136-1941-4

Filmset by Keyspools Ltd, Golborne, Lancs.
Printed in Great Britain by
BAS Printers Limited, Over Wallop, Hampshire

Contents

Colours

Badger: From white to deep cream with a black centre.

Black: Usually dyed as a perfect black. Very rare in nature.

Bronze: Of bronze, or deeply tanned appearance.

Brown: The most sought-after is of a medium shade, but browns may vary from pale ginger to a strong brown.

Coachman Brown: Mahogany brown. Used in the dressing of a Royal Coachman.

Chinchilla: The colour is the opposite of the *Grizzly* that comes from a Plymouth Rock cock: it is white or cream, with black or dark grey stripes. Origin in India or China.

Coch-y-Bonddu: Rust-coloured with a black centre. The tips of the feathers are black, which distinguishes them from the *Furnace*.

Cream: Easy to find. Actually of a dirty white colour. Shades from pale to dark through gingery.

Cree: Fairly rare. Tri-colour – cream or pale ginger with a red or dark grey or black. If this hackle is used, a *Grizzly* can be omitted from the dressing of an Adams.

Dun: This term denotes a whole range of shades from grey-blue to bronze. There are never two hackles of the same shade. The most popular of this family is the *Blue Dun*, q.v.

Blue Dun: Rarely found but much sought after; an even mid-grey without bronze glints. In this context 'blue' means a bluish grey similar to that of a hare's coat.

Dark Blue Dun: Rarely found.

Light Blue Dun: Dyed.

Iron Blue Dun: Dyed.

Medium Blue Dun: Dyed. This replaces natural *Blue Dun* in tying artificials.

Pale Blue Dun: Pale grey-blue with a touch of blue difficult to see. The touch of blue is more visible in the dyed variety and gives it a mottled appearance.

Slate Blue Dun: Rarely found.

Watery Blue Dun: Dyed.

Bronze Dun: The most common and the finest in quality of all natural Duns. Greyish-brown in colour with a touch of bronze. The colour is not bright, but blotchy or mottled.

Honey Dun: These hackles are cream with a mouse-grey centre.

Olive Dun: The natural colour is similar to that of the *Bronze Dun* but there is a glint of dark green.

Rusty Dun: Mouse grey with a touch of reddish-brown, mottled.

Furnace: The hackles are rust-brown with a black centre. Generally of inferior quality.

Ginger: A rusty shade.

Ginger Variant: A golden ginger with red bars, very expensive.

Ginger Grizzly (Light *Ginger Variant*): The hackle is dark cream with horizontal stripes of ginger.

Dark Ginger: Pale brown with a touch of red.

Light Ginger: Has golden glints and the centre is occasionally black.

Grizzly: Dark grey or black with white stripes, from the domestic Plymouth Rock cock of North America and also from one type of Indian cock (although the latter is usually of poor quality). The best Plymouth Rock hackles are much sought-after and very costly.

Honey: In the golden ginger range of colour but of a shining honey shade.

Terminology

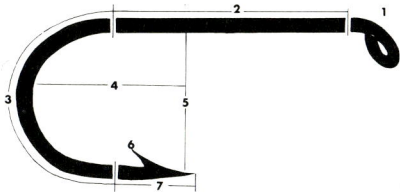

Hook

1 – Eye	5 – Gap
2 – Shank	6 – Barb
3 – Bend	7 – Point
4 – Throat	

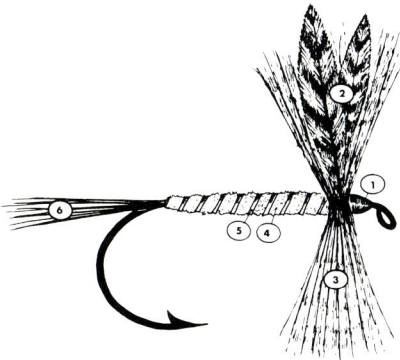

Dry Fly

1 – Head	4 – Body
2 – Wings	5 – Ribbing
3 – Hackles	6 – Tail

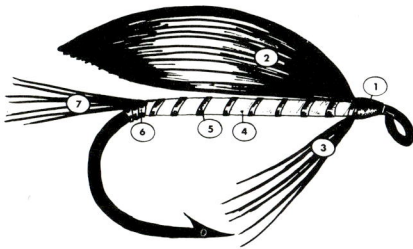

Wet Fly

1 – Head	5 – Ribbing
2 – Wing	6 – Tag
3 – Throat	7 – Tail
4 – Body	

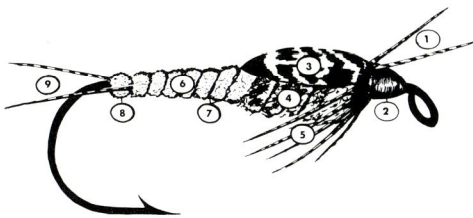

Nymph

1 – Antennae (feelers)	5 – Legs
	6 – Body
2 – Head	7 – Ribbing
3 – Wing case	8 – Butt
4 – Thorax	9 – Tails

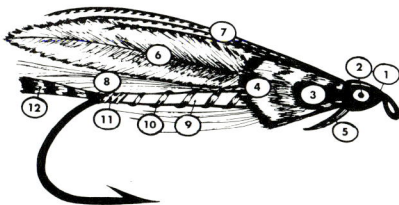

Streamer

1 – Head	7 – Topping
2 – Eye	8 – Underwings
3 – Cheeks	9 – Body
4 – Shoulders	10 – Ribbing
5 – Throat	11 – Tags
6 – Wings	12 – Tail

Chapter One

EQUIPMENT

EQUIPMENT

There are many fly-dressers who never use a vice or a bobbin-holder or even a pair of hackle pliers when tying flies; I would not advise you to follow their example. The tools and instruments I am about to recommend are not costly and they do simplify the task of the fly-tyer, whether novice or expert.

Is it possible to contemplate fly-dressing without a suitable place to work in? The answer is 'yes', but it is much easier and more satisfying if one can find a corner where work in progress can remain undisturbed and equipment can be set up. For this, a table or bench rigid enough to accept a vice and a light is of first importance.

Bench

Part of my bench is devoted to the housing of my materials and tools. The pegboard is used to accommodate scissors, bobbin-holders, pliers, specialist tools and even some spools. The type of bobbin-holder seen on top of the cabinet is useful for keeping threads and silks in order. The cabinet with transparent drawers is ideal for storing hooks, flies and even insects in bottles containing a dilute formaldehyde solution.

A desk with drawers, or a table 1 metre wide, 1.35 metres long and 0.70 metres high makes an ideal bench. However, it is possible to make do with a portable mini-bench like the one shown below.

Vice

This instrument, if of good quality, will last a lifetime. Look for a vice with adjustable jaws of

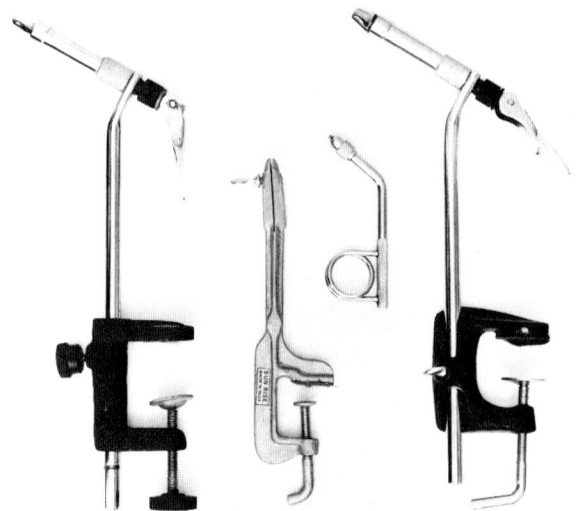

Sunrise 'Double A'   Sunrise 'B'   Thompson 'B'

hardened steel, fitted with a release lever. The central stem should also be adjustable in height and free to rotate to accommodate both right-handers and left-handers.

Bobbin-holders

Versions of the bobbin-holder range from the simple to the complex, but the basic purpose of this piece of equipment is to hold the spool whilst allowing it to turn and so release an even delivery of the required length of silk or nylon during fly-tying.

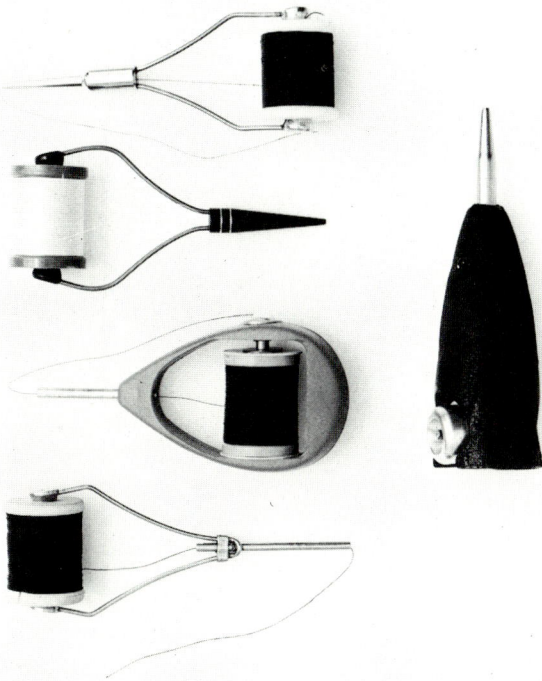

Bodkins

The bodkin is used for dubbing, or wrapping, the fur round the fly body; for applying glue or varnish to the head, and for forming certain knots.

Hackle pliers

There is a wide range of hackle pliers on the market. They are manufactured by various firms, are modestly priced and make the job of positioning hackles much easier. They are made in different sizes; a set of two or three pairs will cope with all the hackles you need to tie.

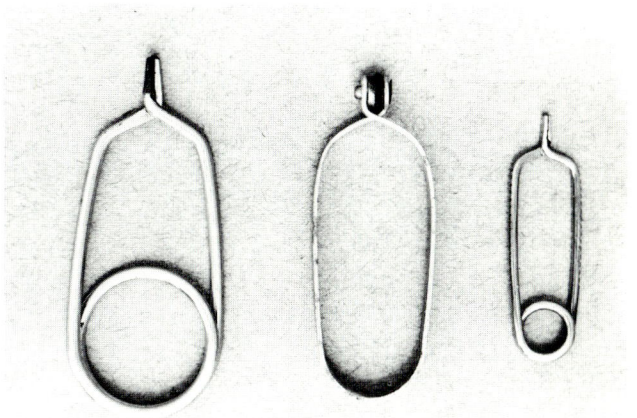

Scissors

Whilst it is possible to use a razor-blade, the serious fly-dresser equips himself with a well-sharpened pair of straight-bladed scissors for the main body of the work and a pair with curved blades for finishing off. Features to look for in a pair of scissors are durability, a clean cut, sharp points and a comfortable grip.

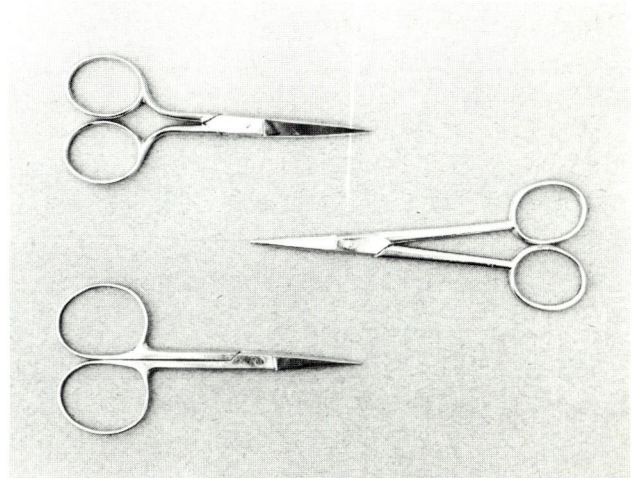

Half-hitch tool

This is an invaluable accessory, used for tying half-hitches at different stages. Fitted with a needle at one end it can be made into a dual-purpose tool and used for dubbing.

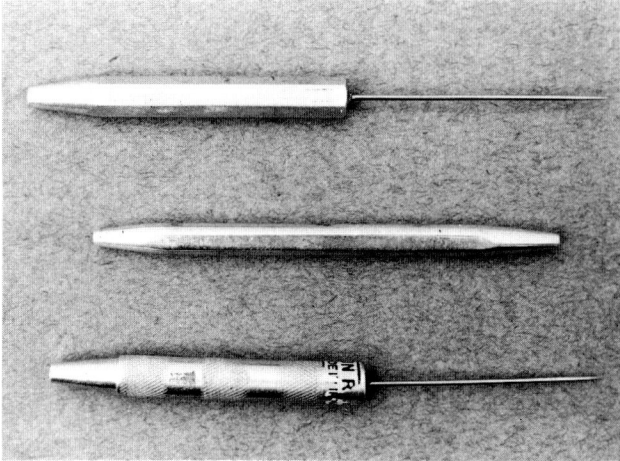

Whip-finish tool

This tool, which some dressers find indispensable, is used for rapid finishing.

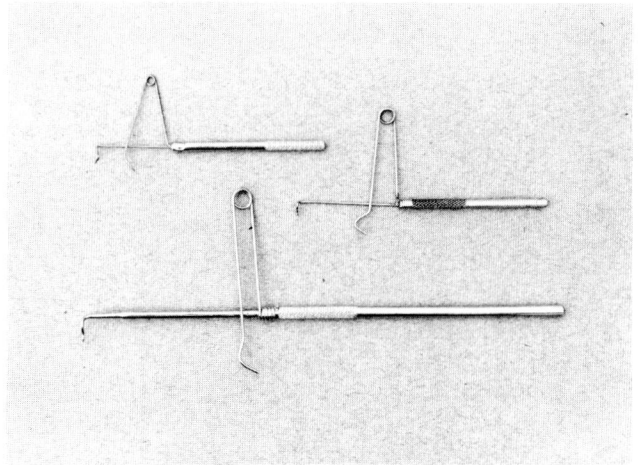

QUILLS

FLANK FEATHERS

PEACOCK (eye & sword) &
PHEASANT TAIL

STRICH

PECCARY

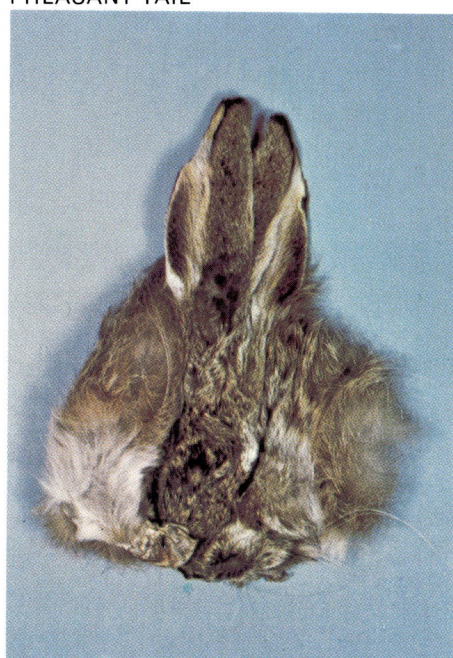

HARE'S MASK

UR AND SKINS

TAILS

HACKLE CAPES

JUNGLE COCK CAPE

TYING SILKS

FLOSS SILKS

TINSELS

VARNISHES

WAXES

Patterns

LACK NOSE DACE

MAGOG SMELT

GREY GHOST

ENDRICKSON NYMPH

COACHMAN

BIVISIBLE

LUE DUN (SPIDER)

HENDRICKSON DRY FLY

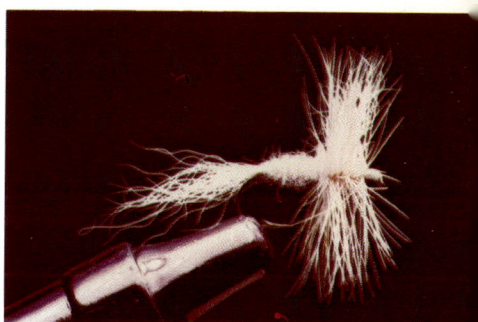

WHITE WULFF

J. V. CADDIS

JAC'S RED STONE

JAC'S MARCH BROWN

ORNBURG

JOLIETTE HOPPER

MUDDLER

Specials

HORNBURG
JOLIETTE HOPPER

MUDDLER
WHITE MARABOU MUDDLER

Streamers

BLACK NOSE DACE
MICKEY FINN
SILVER SHINER

MAGOG SMELT
NINE THREE
SUPERVISOR

GREY GHOST
BLACK GHOST
GREEN GHOST

ROYAL COACHMAN
DARK SPRUCE FLY
LIGHT SPRUCE FLY

Wet Flies

DARK HENDRICKSON
DARK CAHILL
LIGHT CAHILL
LIGHT HENDRICKSON
QUILL GORDON

COACHMAN
BLACK GNAT
BLUE DUN
BLUE WINGED OLIVE
DARK MONTREAL

GINGER QUILL
GOLD RIBBED HARE'S EAR
LEAD WING COACHMAN
MARCH BROWN
PARMACHENE BELLE

Dry Flies

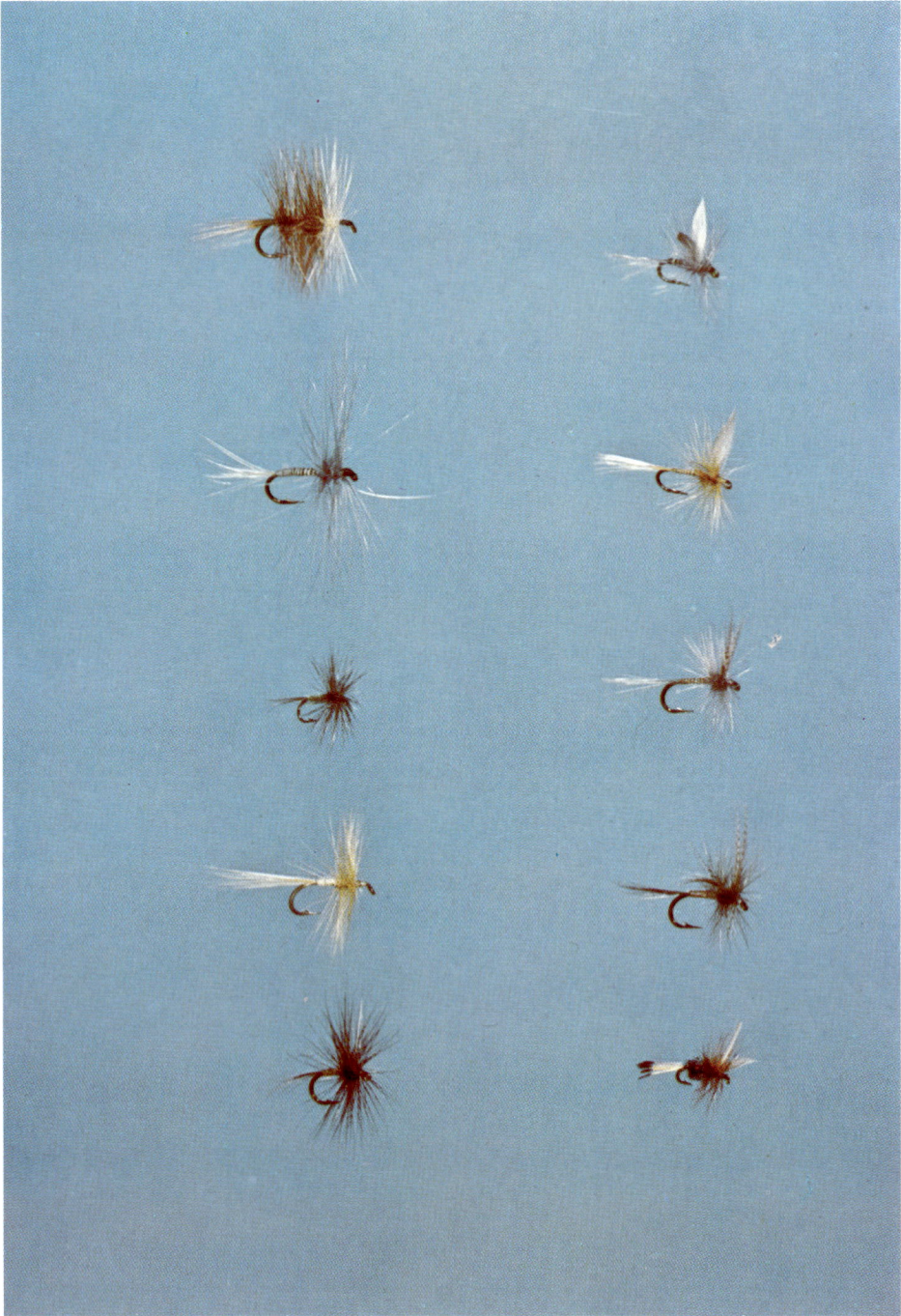

BROWN BIVISIBLE
BLUE DUN (SPIDER)
BLUE WINGED OLIVE
CREAM VARIANT
DUN VARIANT

BLUE QUILL
GINGER QUILL
QUILL GORDON
RED QUILL
ROYAL COACHMAN

HENDRICKSON
ADAMS
BLUE DUN
BLACK GNAT
DARK CAHILL

GREY FOX (FLICK)
GREEN DRAKE (COFFIN FLY)
LIGHT CAHILL
LIGHT HENDRICKSON
MARCH BROWN

WHITE WULFF
AUSABLE WULFF
BLACK WULFF
BLONDE WULFF

BROWN WULFF
GREY WULFF
GRIZZLY WULFF
ROYAL WULFF

Nymphs

JAC'S MARCH BROWN
BLUE QUILL NYMPH
HARE'S EAR
HENDRICKSON

MARCH BROWN
AMERICAN MARCH BROWN
FLICK'S MARCH BROWN
ZUG BUG

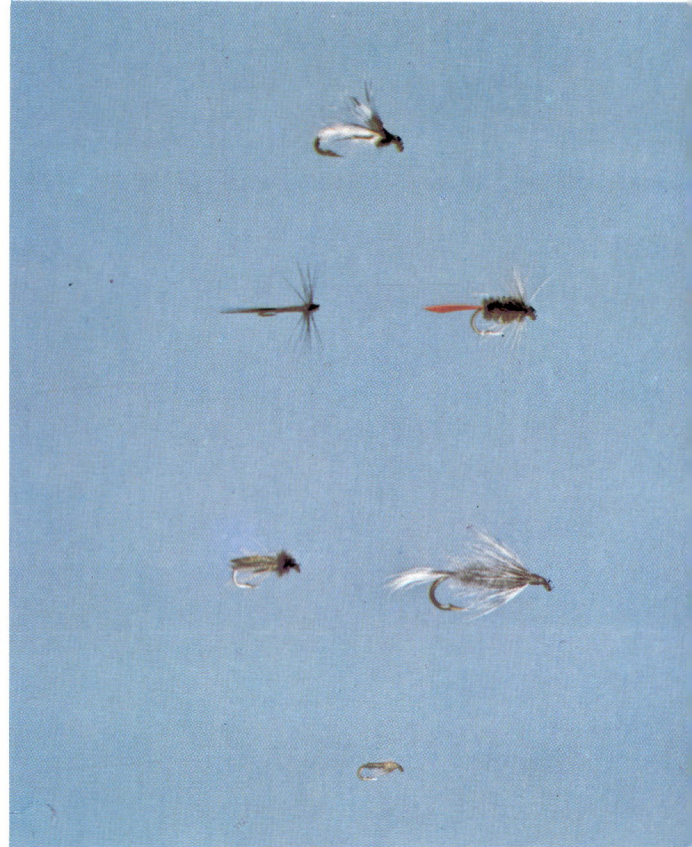

S. J. V. CADDIS
BLACK MIDGE   BROWN HACKLE
GREEN CADDIS PUPA   GREY NYMPH
MIDGE PUPA

JAC'S RED STONE

JAC'S GREY STONE
JAC'S BROWN STONE
JAC'S BLACK STONE

LARGE BLACK STONE FLY

Chapter Two

THE MATERIALS

MATERIALS

Not so long ago, the slightest deviation from the original pattern for a particular fly was considered sacrilege. The art of dressing obliged members of the fly-fishing fraternity to dress flies by using the feathers of exotic birds, or the fur of rare animals. But fly-dressers have now come to realise that flies do not possess magic powers and that the substitution of certain materials for others has no detrimental effect on the positive response of the trout to a delicate and well-tied fly.

However, some flies require the use of materials with quite specific textures, lustres and behavioural qualities. These requirements are an essential part of many patterns and the serious fly-dresser should respect these guidelines when choosing alternative materials.

Hackles

Hackles are the small, lance-shaped feathers which come from the neck area of the bird; the quality of these feathers determines their usage in fly-dressing. Today, we classify hackles in four groups: hackles for dry-flies, hackles for wet-flies, hackles for nymphs and hackles for streamers. This same classification also applies to saddle hackles.

The dry-type hackle has very few fibres on its stem. Quills are shiny and rigid.

Both the wet-type and nymph-type hackle are soft and the stems have many fibres.

The streamer-type hackle is similar to the dry-type but is much broader.

Feathers

Nowadays, I know of no bird which cannot contribute something to fly-dressing. Goose, duck, turkey, pheasant, partridge, grouse, quail, crow, pigeon and chicken all offer wing, tail and other feathers for the making of dry and wet fly wings and for the wing-cases of nymphs and stoneflies.

The blue teal, the pintail, the mallard, the crested duck, the mandarin duck, the shoveller, the American whistler and the crowned sawbill provide flank and breast feathers for making the wings and tails of several popular flies.

Ostrich, emu, peacock, condor and heron provide quills for making bodies, toppings, tails and ribbing.

The marabou gives its feathers and the cock its saddle hackles for the winging of streamers.

Fur

Most of the wild animals to be found in Britain provide fur suitable for fly-dressing. Apart from these we also use the tail of the 'Impali' calf or 'Kiptail', the skins of the mountain goat and of the opossum, the stiff hairs of the peccary, the mantle of the polar bear and the coat of the leopard.

Several dry fly patterns require the hair of deer, caribou, elk, marmot, badger, lynx, monkey or polar bear as well as hairs from the tails of calves and squirrels to be used for wings.

These same hairs make excellent 'bucktail' wings, as do hairs from the baboon, fox, mink, Siberian wolf, skunk and roebuck.

Silks

When I first started fly-dressing, silk was the only thread used. I still use some silk in shades which are not available in nylon. Despite all the advantages of nylon, silk still has its place even where this is purely a question of tradition.

For many years the firm of Pearsall has been manufacturing silk for the fly-dresser, and their Gossamer and Naples tying silks and their Marabou and Stout Floss body silks are world famous. Gossamer silk is suitable for all sizes of trout flies and low-water salmon flies. However, some tiers prefer something a little stronger for large flies and for these Naples silk is admirably suited. The colour range is quite extensive, although the Naples range is a little more limited.

Tinsels

Nowadays we are familiar with tinsels which come in flat, oval or embossed form and in gilt or silver finish. They are available in three thicknesses: fine, medium and coarse, and are used in the dressing of various flies. All, therefore, have their place on your work-bench.

Soon we shall have yarns which look like the latest tinsels but have the additional advantage of not tarnishing. There is already on the market a material which is destined to replace lamé in the making of tinsel streamer bodies. It is even possible to use a 'Mylar' in tube form to make the body of a Black Nose Dace, Mickey Finn or Silver Shiner, patterns for which are given in the text which follows.

Floss silks
These silks consist of several strands of silk, nylon, rayon or cellulite. I like Pearsall's silks but some fly patterns require the texture of marabou silk.

Floss silks consisting of silk strands are ideal for making the bodies of certain streamers, whilst those which contain cellulite react in an acetone solution and can thus be moulded to any required shape. This is essential for the imitation of the bodies of certain nymphs and streamers.

These silks are available in more than twenty different colours.

Varnishes
The fly-dresser has access to a wide range of varnishes which are used for sealing the final knot and for consolidating the head of the fly. Quick-drying transparent varnish is used to preserve hackles, the wings of dry flies and those of the Hornburg; it can also be used to hold together and protect split jungle cock feathers.

Wax (Resin)
The resin used for preparing silk for dressing is extracted from pine and fir trees. Mixed with beeswax, it facilitates the dubbing of fur or hair used on the fly body.

Wax cakes need softening with a little turpentine before using. Some fly-dressers heat the wax in a container placed close to a candle while they work at the bench, then coat the silk with the aid of a little paint-brush.

E. Veniard offer a liquid wax which I use when working with a soft fur which contains no coarse hairs. It can be applied with a paint-brush or bodkin.

When the fur includes coarse hairs or has a difficult pile, I use Thompson's wax. It is very sticky, but after coating the silk the fingers can be wiped clean with a turpentine-soaked cloth.

Mustad Hooks
(Reproduced actual size)

No 79580

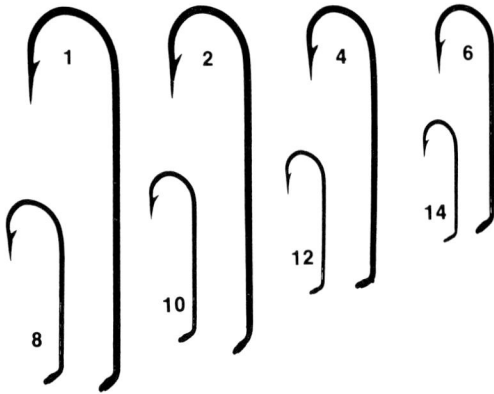

No 3665-A

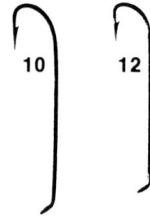

No 9671

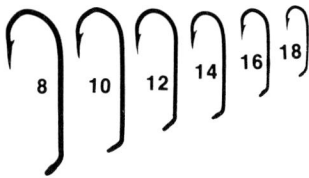

No 3906

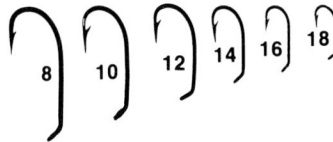

No 3906 B

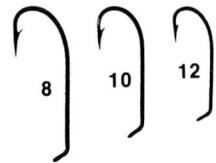

No 94840

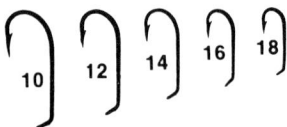

No 94833

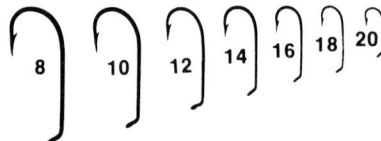

No 94845

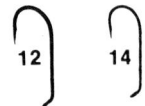

No 94840

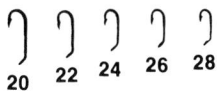

No 540-L

No 94842

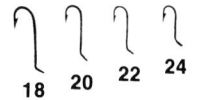

Chapter Three

BASIC METHODS

BASIC METHODS

Before embarking on a detailed study of the basics, I would like to explain one or two techniques which make all the difference between a high-quality fly and one which disintegrates after the first few casts.

While dressing is in progress it is essential that the silk remains taut at all times. Neither the bobbin-holder nor the hackle pliers are capable of creating sufficient tension, so I suggest that you tie a half-hitch knot after each stage of construction. These knots will ensure the stability of the wound tinsel as well as that of all other materials used in dubbing. There is the added advantage of their increasing the overall strength.

Two or three half-hitches in a row do not give the necessary strength for finishing off the fly. Always use the whip finish, which is basically the method used to bind the rings of your fly rod.

Waxing the silk or nylon (if it is not already waxed) will facilitate the addition of materials for dubbing the fly.

Stripping a peacock's quill

The operation of preparing a peacock's tail feather prior to its use as the tail or body sections of a fly is really quite simple, although the preparation varies according to the type of fly to be dressed.

If it is to be used for dressing the Quill Gordon fly, do not hesitate to plunge the 'eye' of the tail feather into a saucer of concentrated bleach. The fibres will immediately begin to disintegrate and the operation will be complete in less than a minute. Remove the feather and place it in a jar containing a solution of water with a spoonful of bicarbonate of soda; this solution will halt the chemical action of the bleach. After one or two minutes, rinse the eye feather in cold water.

You would do well to remember that the quills are very fragile and break extremely easily. It helps to soak them in tepid water before use.

A peacock's feather can also be stripped by passing it between the thumb and index finger, at the same time applying a certain amount of pressure with the thumbnail.

You will achieve the same effect by placing the feather on a smooth polished surface, pressing a bodkin across it, then pulling on the feather.

I have used all these methods but generally find it best to use an eraser to eliminate the fibres. When dressing a Quill Gordon fly, I soak the stripped quills in peroxide for eight hours to bleach them. To soften them, whilst I work I leave them in a mollifying solution.

Method 1

THE INITIAL KNOT

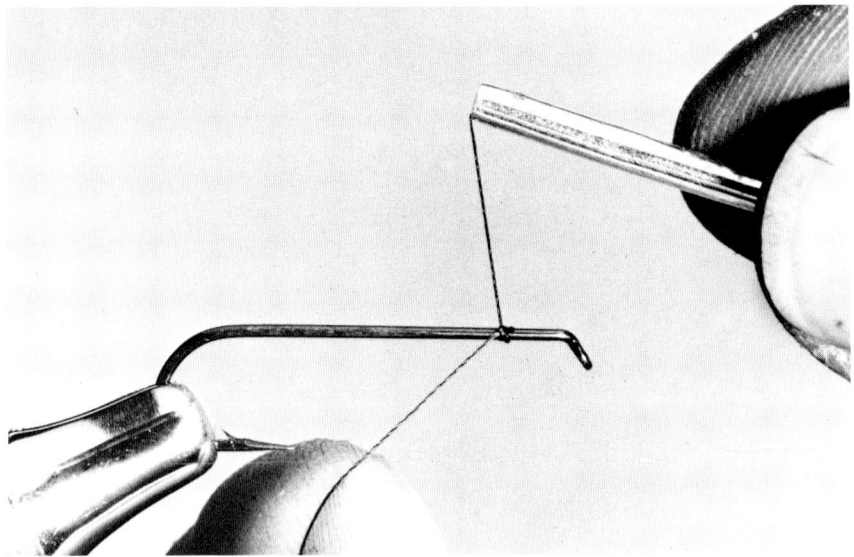

1.1

Hold the end of the silk between the thumb and index finger of the left hand. With the right hand pass the thread from the bobbin-holder over the shank at a point about 5 mm from its eye.

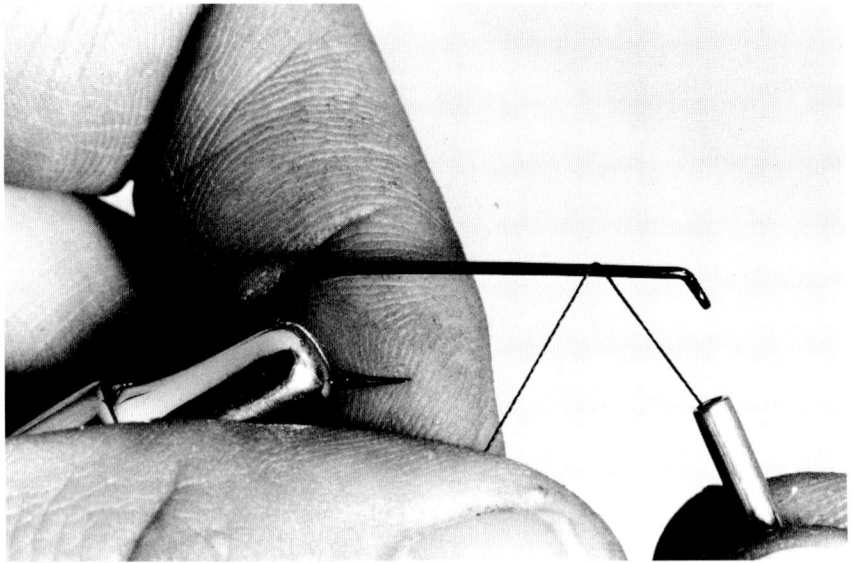

1.2

Wind the thread round the shank, working from front to back and moving towards the left, at the same time binding the end of the silk held in the left hand under these first turns.

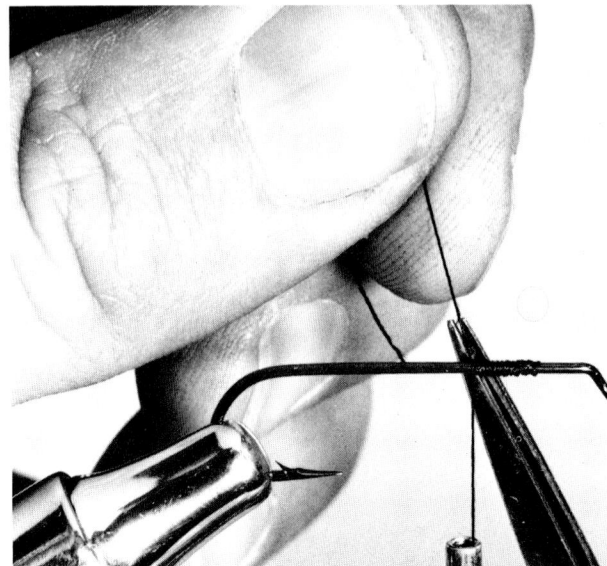

1.3

When five or six turns have been made, make a half-hitch and cut off the protruding end of the silk neatly with the scissors.

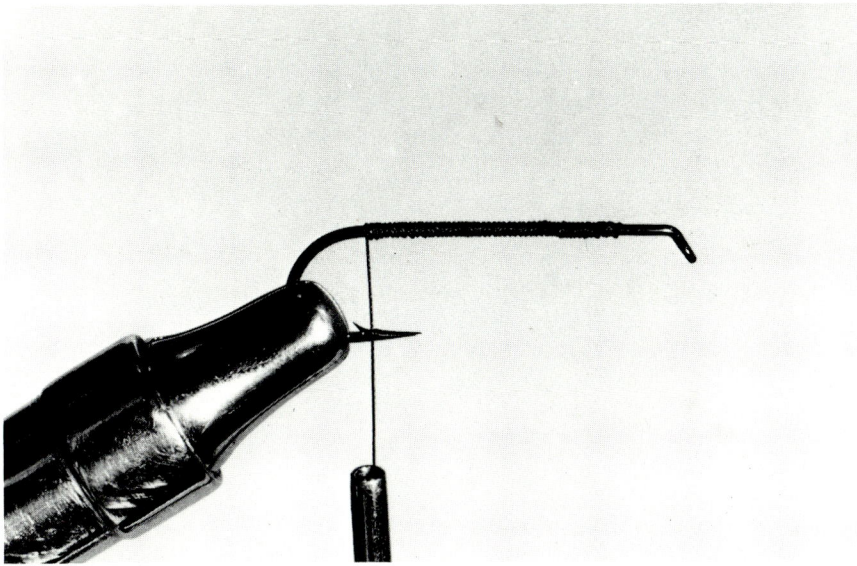

1.4
Pick up the bobbin-holder again with the right hand and continue to wind the thread towards the left in tight turns, taking great care not to overlap.

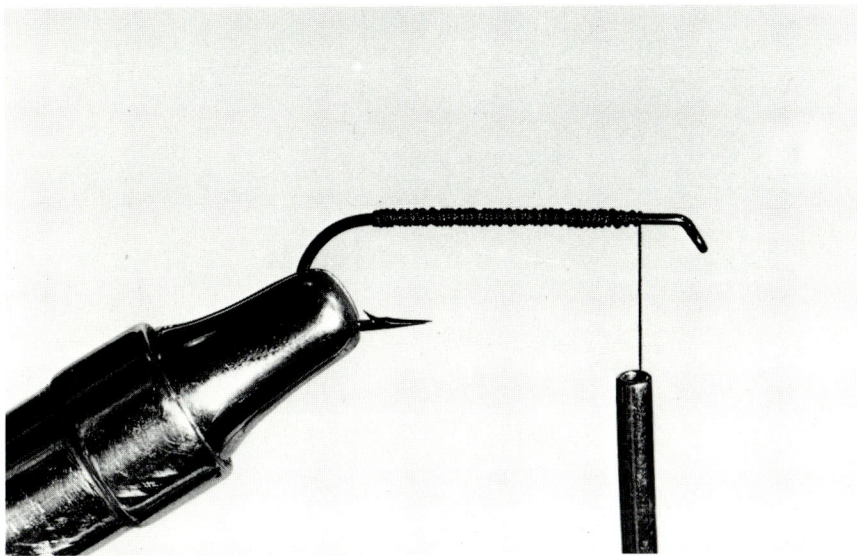

1.5
When you reach the point where the bend of the hook begins you can either continue with the tying in of the tail or return towards the eye, winding evenly. Finish with a half-hitch.

Method 2

WINGS MADE FROM FEATHERS

2.1
Cut a section 6 mm wide from each of the vanes. Remove these sections from the right and left on the concave side of the feather.

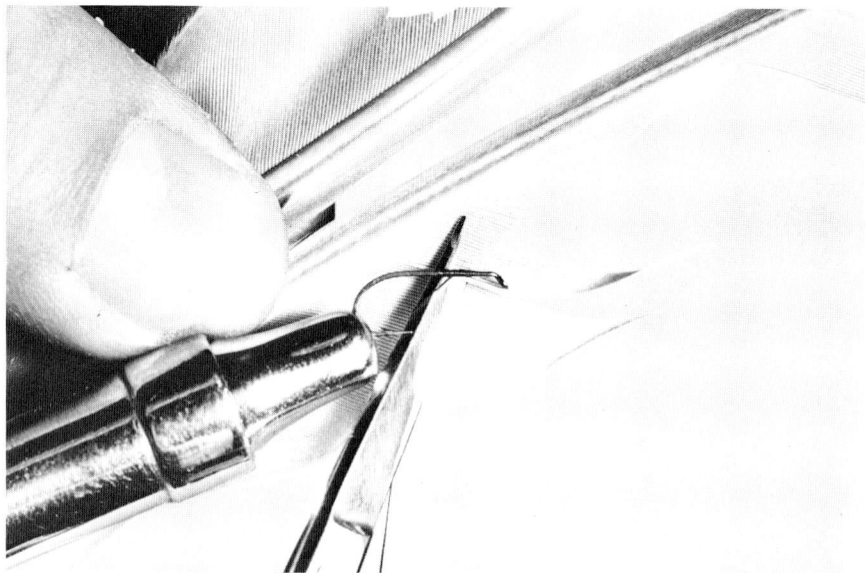

2.2
Align the tips of the sections and hold them between the thumb and index finger of the left hand. They must be the same length as the shank.

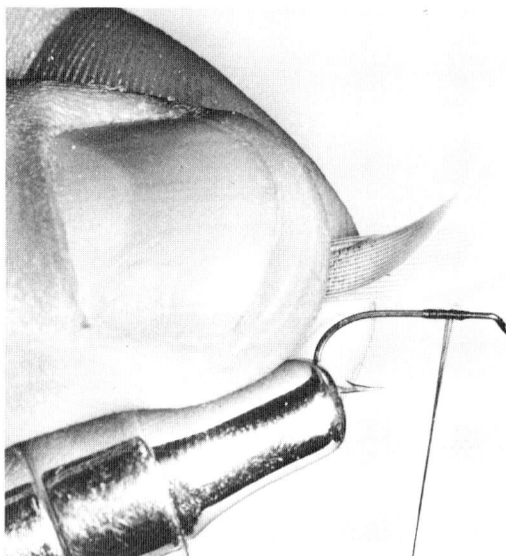

2.3
Position the sections on the shank at the previously selected point of attachment. Pass the thread between the thumb and the index finger and, keeping the silk in place, wind right round the sections.

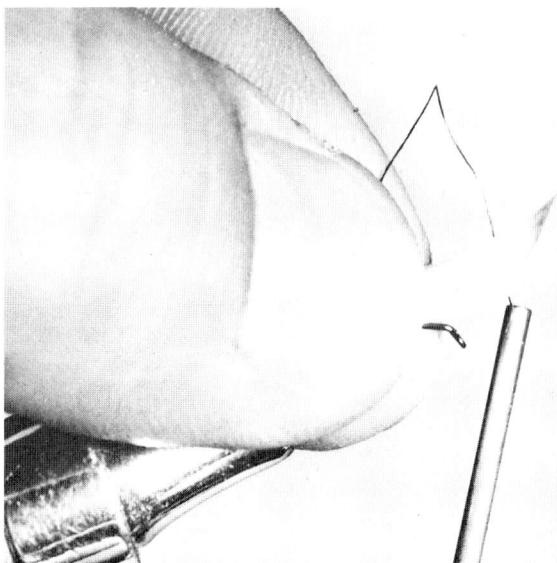

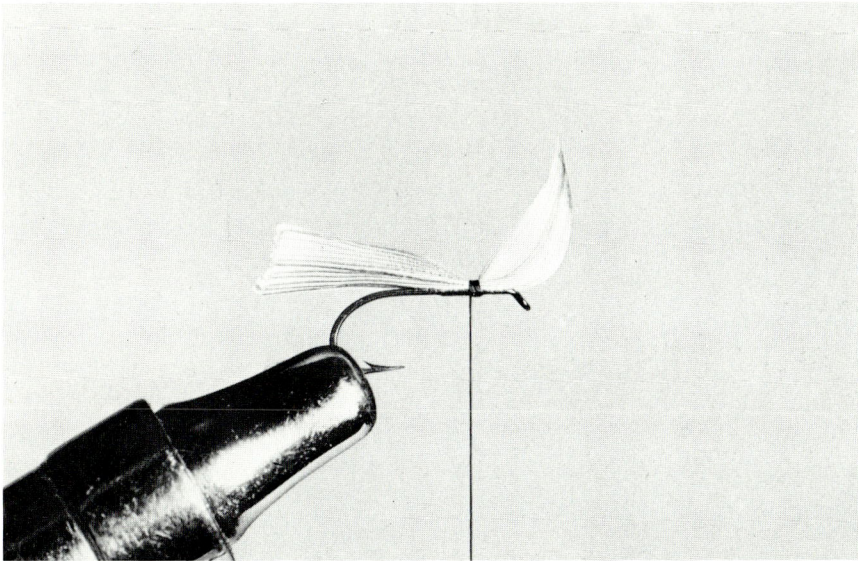

2.4
Pull the silk tight and make three more turns, holding the sections firmly in place. Remove your fingers and make another couple of turns towards the actual base of the wings, i.e. to the left.

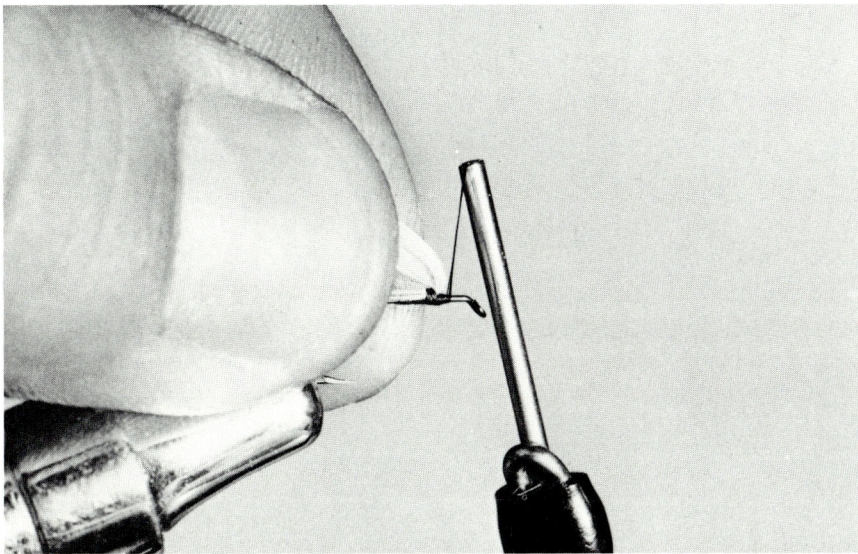

2.5
Pull the wings towards the rear and make four or five turns of silk round the hook (in front of the wings) to form a base.

2.6
Release your grip to allow the wings to resume a vertical position.

2.7

Place the silk behind the wings. Cut the surplus from the sections at an angle. Add a few extra turns of silk and bring forward.

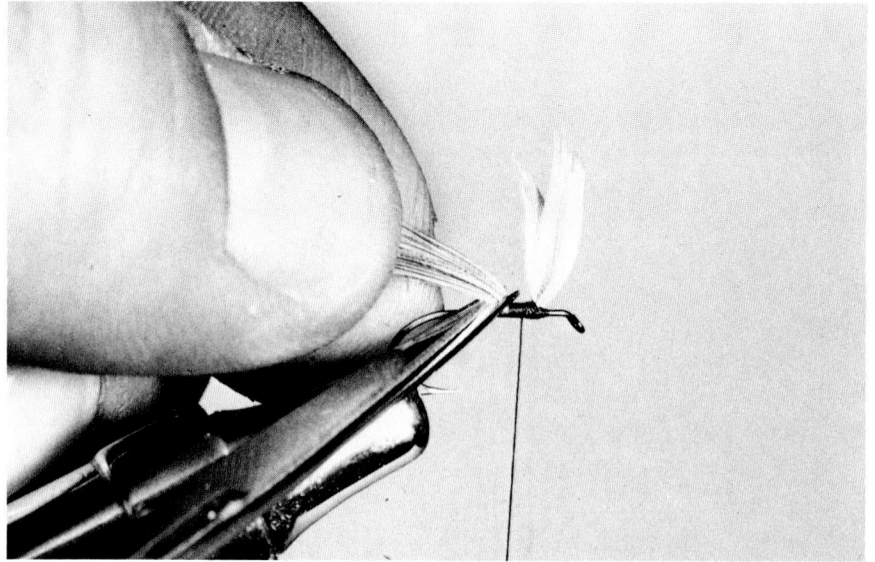

2.8

Using a bodkin or a needle, separate the two wings, being careful to keep them intact.

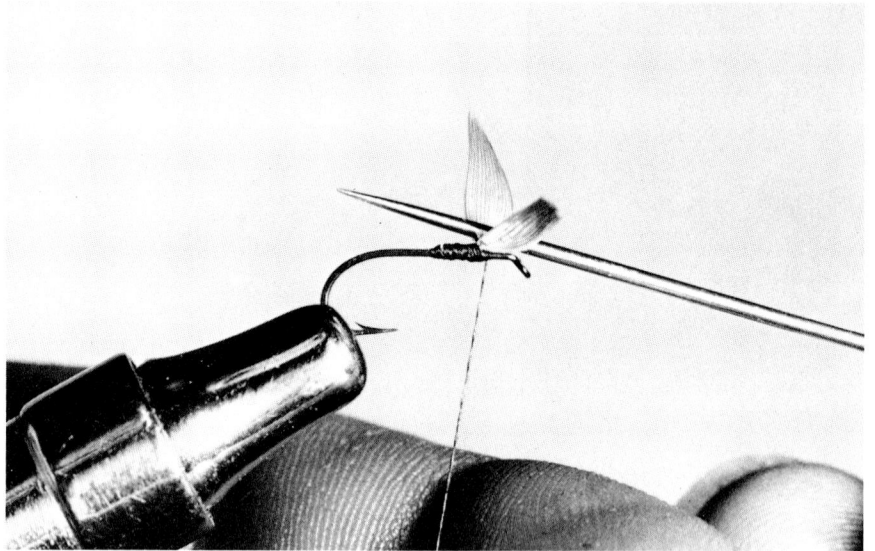

2.9

Pass the silk between the wings towards the rear. Do not exert any tension during this operation.

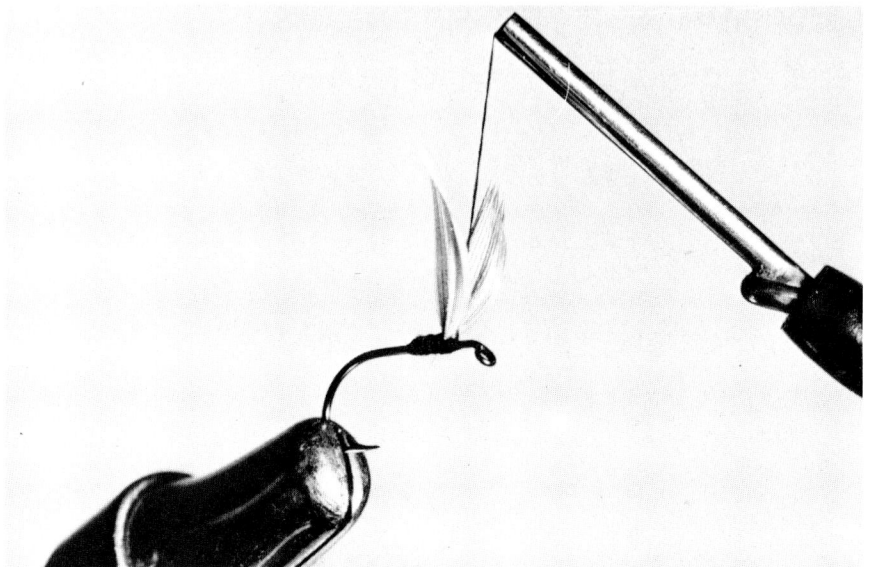

2.10
Feeding out more thread, make a
turn round the base.

2.11
Pass the silk forwards between
the wings.

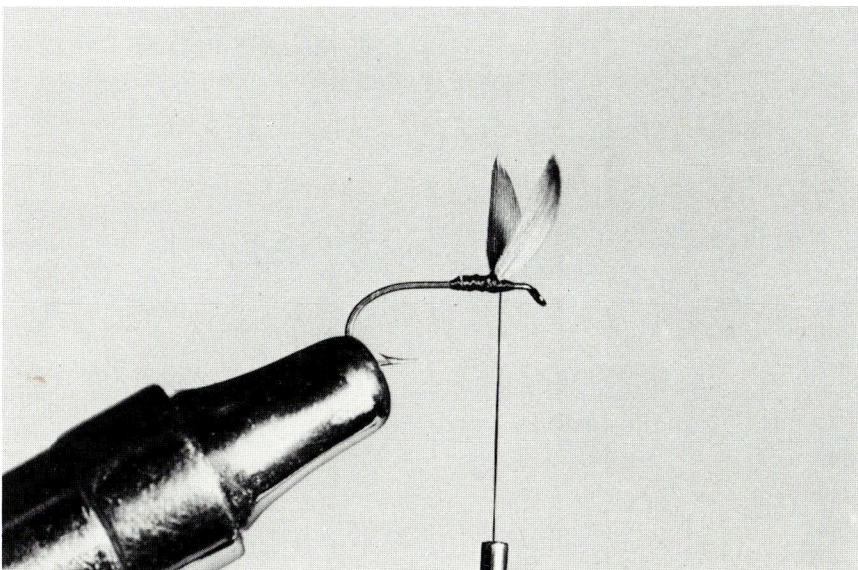

2.12
Hold the wings between the
thumb and index finger and
tighten this figure of eight loop.
Make two extra turns and put a
drop of varnish at the base of the
wings for additional strength.

Method 3

WINGS MADE FROM FLANK FEATHERS

3.1
Select the flank feather of a mallard or crested duck and bend back the fibres which are not married together.

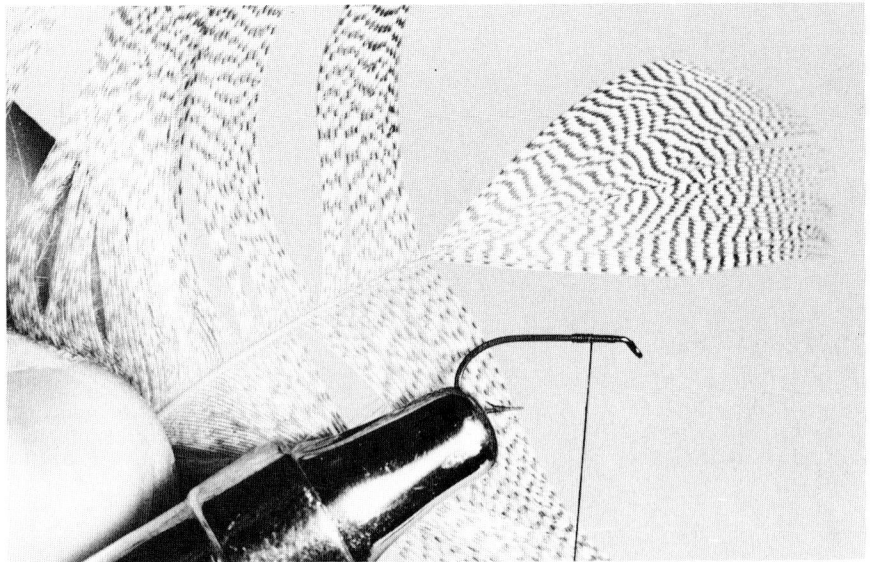

3.2
Press down the stem at the front end of the flank feather and cut off the unusable base.

3.3
Using the thumb and index finger of your right hand, fold the tips of the feather against one another.

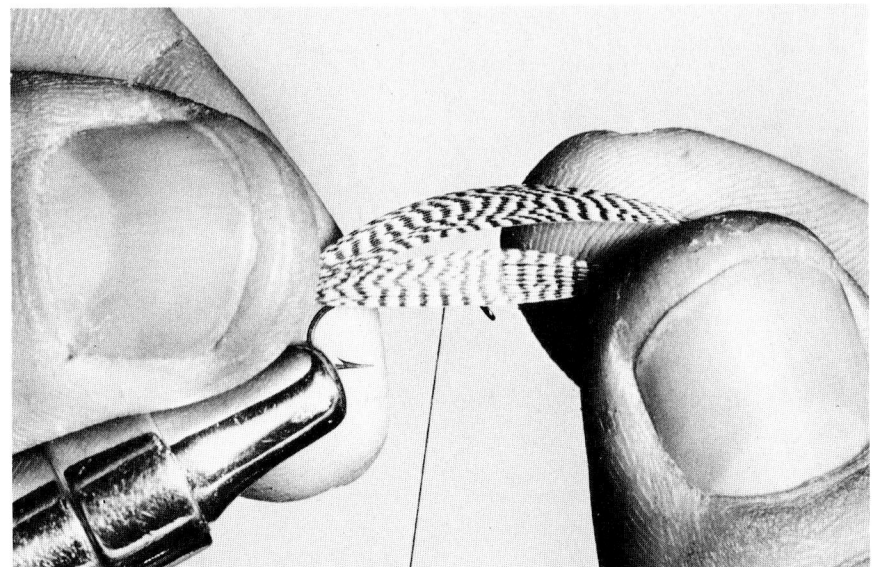

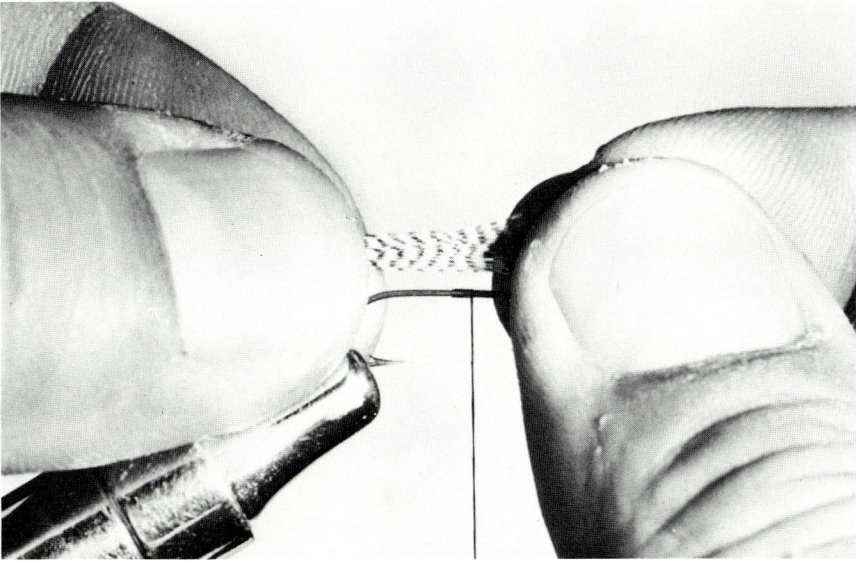

3.4
Bend them again so that, from the rear, their tips incline towards each other.

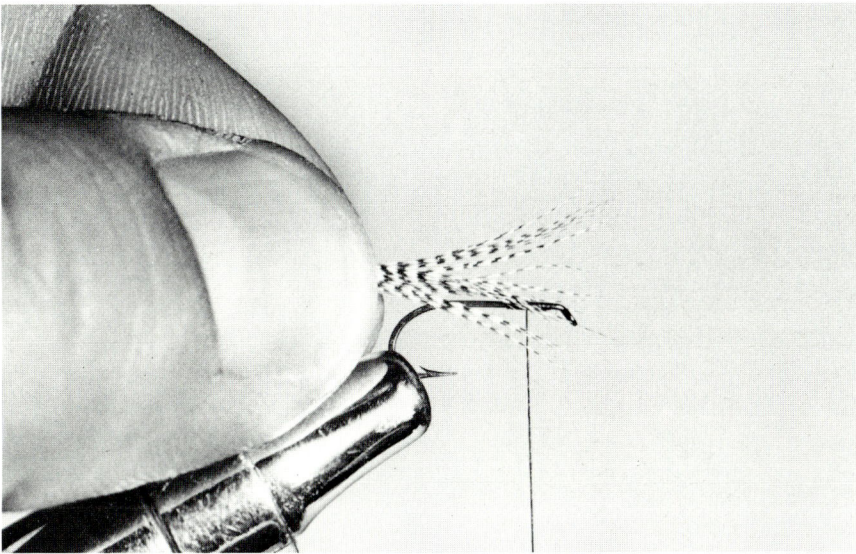

3.5
Measure the fibres against the shank to ensure that they are the same length.

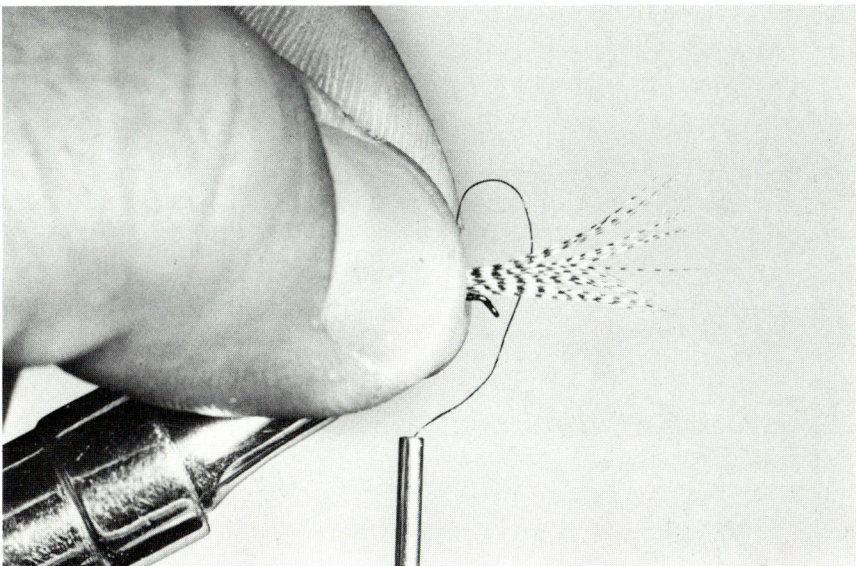

3.6
Reposition the fibres at the point of attachment and with the silk between the thumb and the index finger, make a turn round the fibres.

3.7
Holding the fibres firmly in place, tighten the silk and make three more turns. Then remove the fingers and make one or two extra turns.

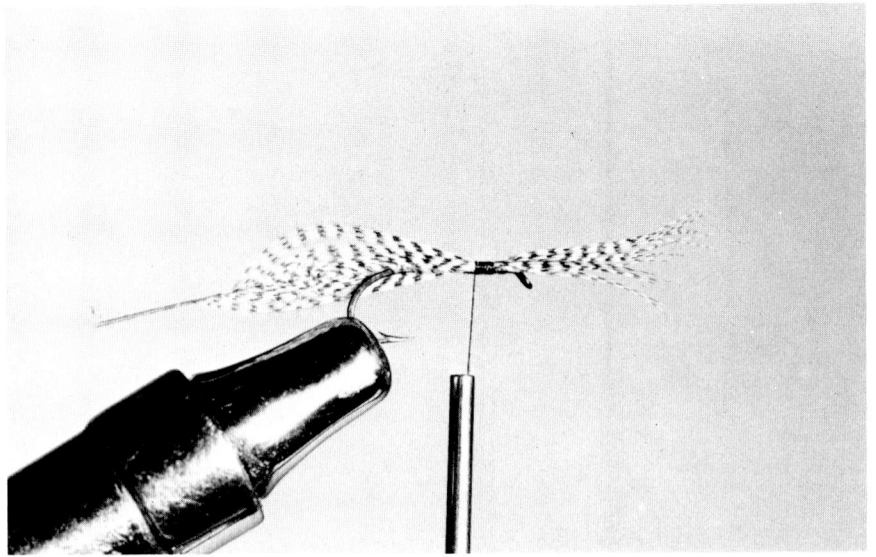

3.8
Bend the fibres backwards and make several overlying turns of silk in front to form a kind of shoulder. This will help to keep the wings upright. Then release your grip and cut off the surplus fibres.

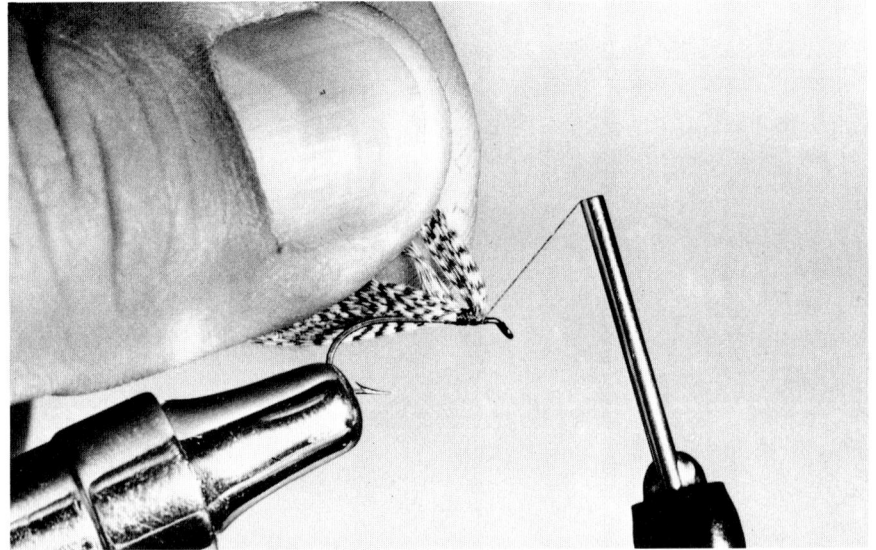

3.9
Using a bodkin, separate the fibres into equal bunches and then grip the bunch on the far side between the thumb and the index finger. Working from the back to the front, pass the silk between the wings.

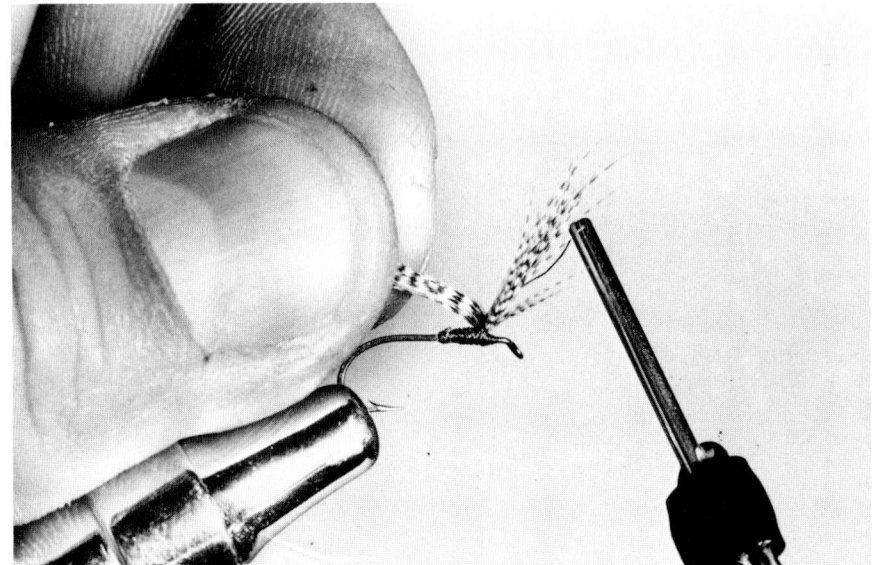

3.10

Repeat this operation with the fibres on the near side, reversing the direction of the silk. If this is not sufficient to hold the wings in a vertical position, make another figure of eight loop.

Once they are in a completely separate and vertical position the wings can be fixed by applying a drop of varnish at the base.

Method 4

**WINGS USING
HACKLE TIPS**

4.1
Choose twin hackles from a
single source and strip the fibres
from the base of the stems.

4.2
Measure the hackles against the
shank of the hook and cut off the
surplus fibres.

4.3
Following the procedure
previously described, with the
thread between the thumb and
the index finger anchor the
hackles firmly to the base.

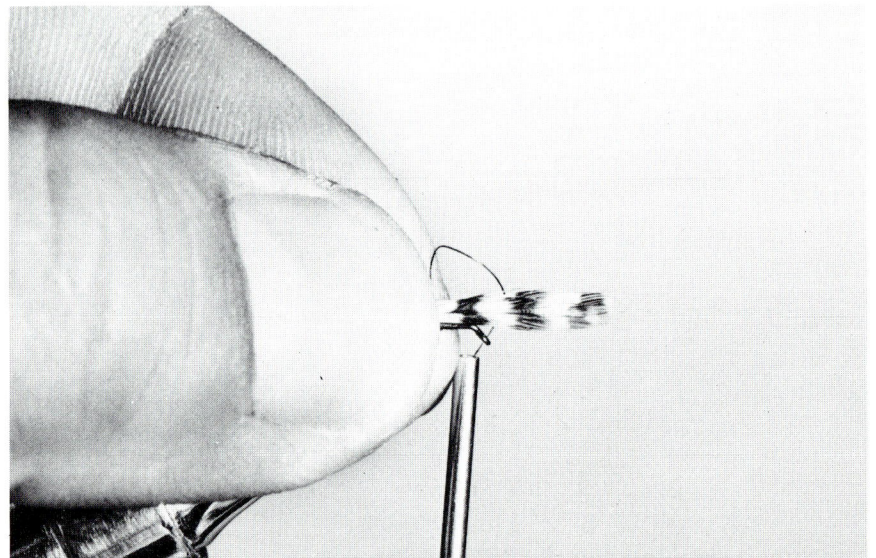

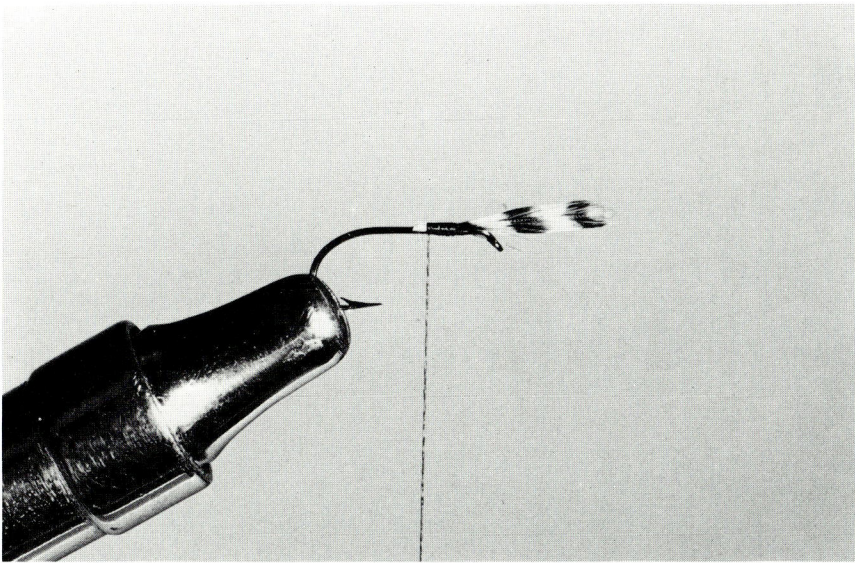

4.4
Take your fingers away and
secure the points by making a
few extra turns with the silk.

4.5
Angle the points backwards and
start to build up a shoulder by
winding several overlying turns
of silk at the base of the wings.

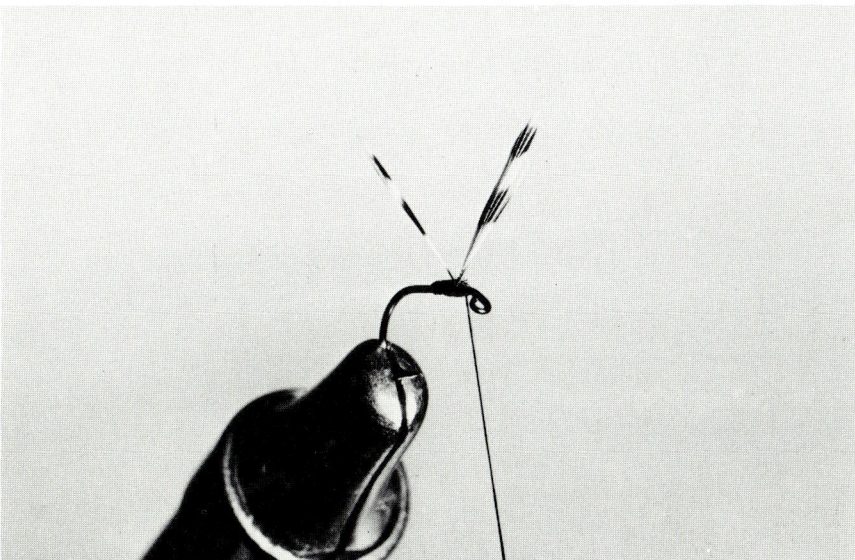

4.6
Using the figure of eight
method, reinforce the wings on
the shank in an upright V
position.

Method 5

WINGS MADE OF HAIR

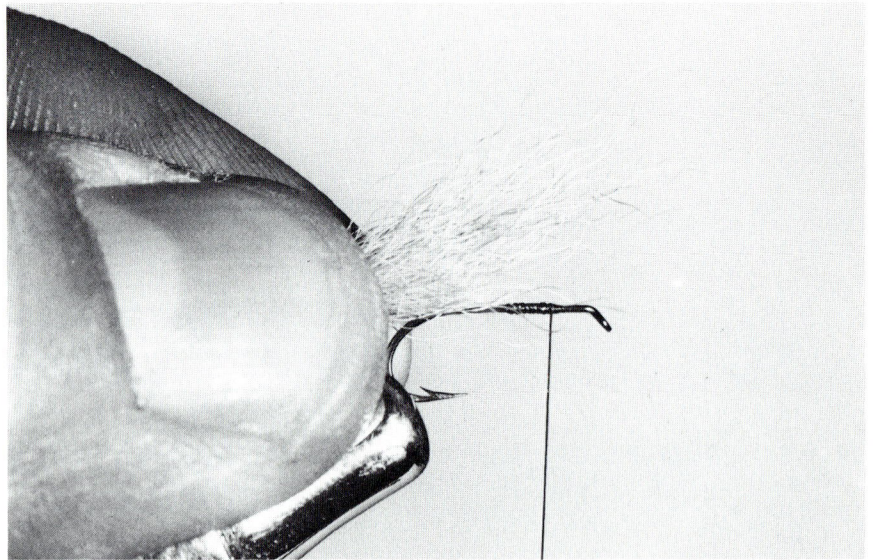

5.1
Take a pinch of hair and measure it against the shank of the hook.

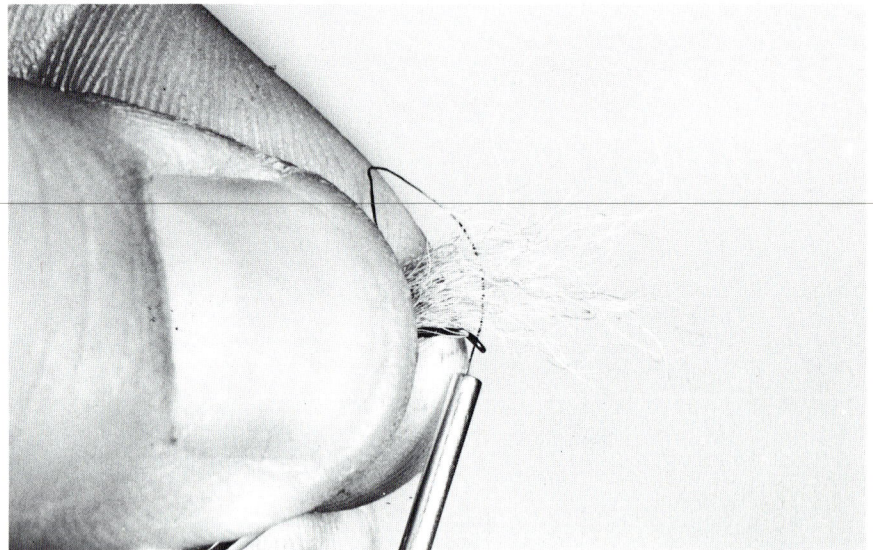

5.2
Anchor the hair firmly to the base, following the procedures already described.

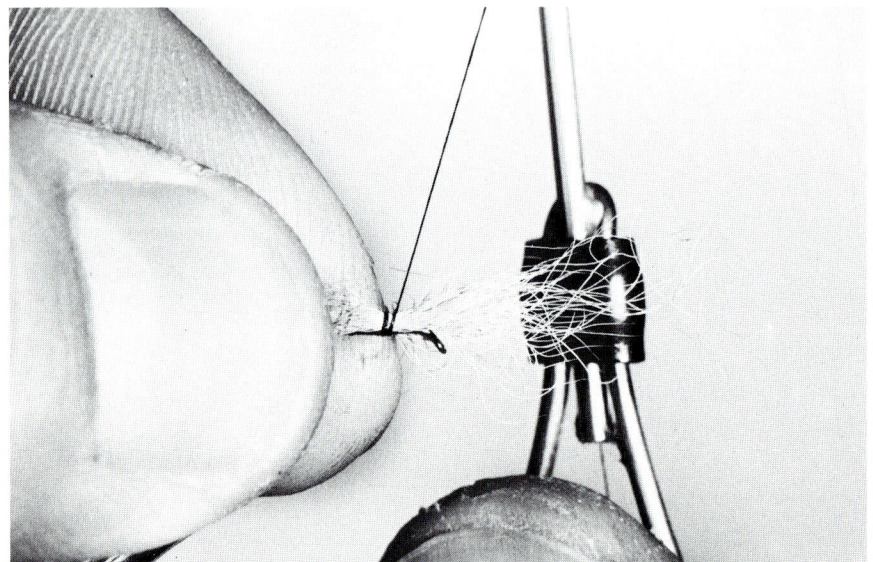

5.3

5.4
Construct a shoulder by winding the silk over and over. Then, using a bodkin, separate the hair into two equal parts. Grip the wing on the far side in the left hand.

5.5

5.6
Proceed with a figure of eight loop which will ensure the vertical position of the wings. Cut off the surplus hair on the shank and apply a drop of varnish to the base of the fork.

Method 6

THE HALF-HITCH KNOT

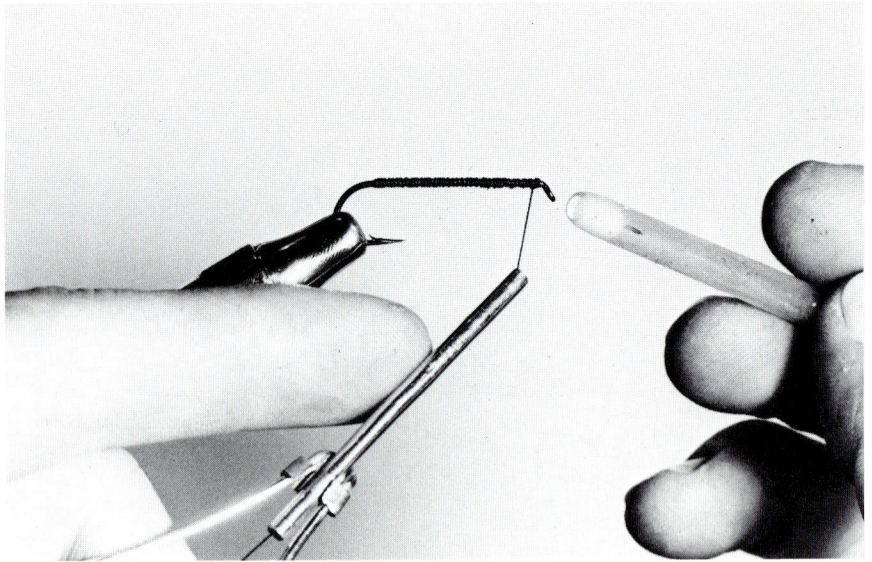

6.1
Place the half-hitch tool close to
the eye of the hook.

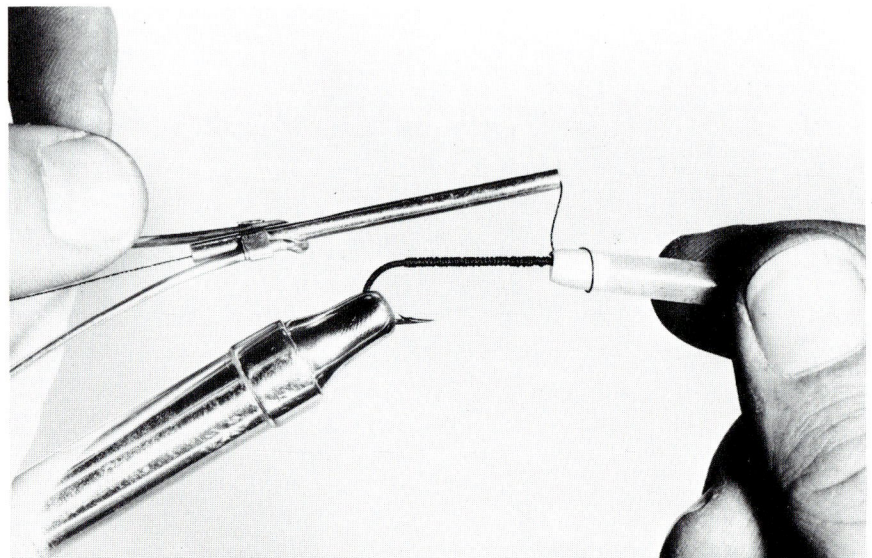

6.2
Pass the silk round the tool,
forming a simple loop.
Manipulate the tool so as to
cross the two ends of the loop.

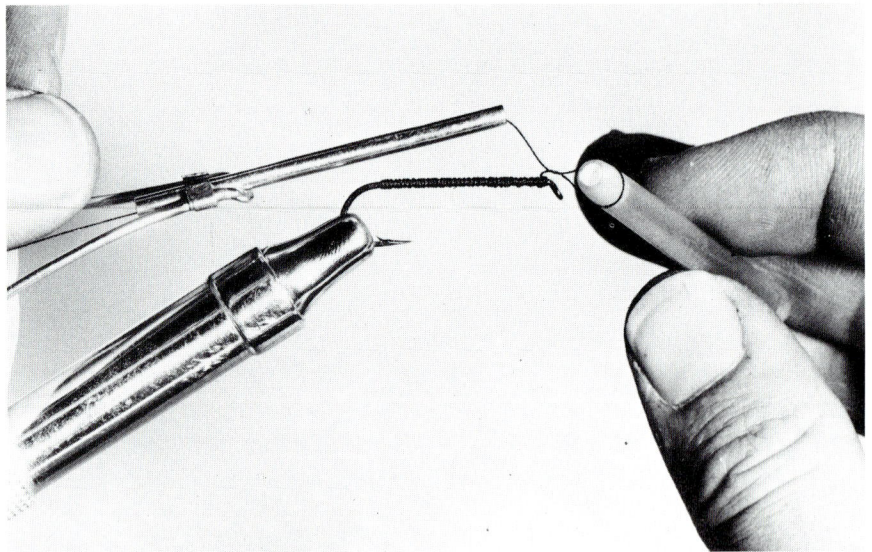

6.3
Insert the eye of the hook into
the hole at the end of the tool.

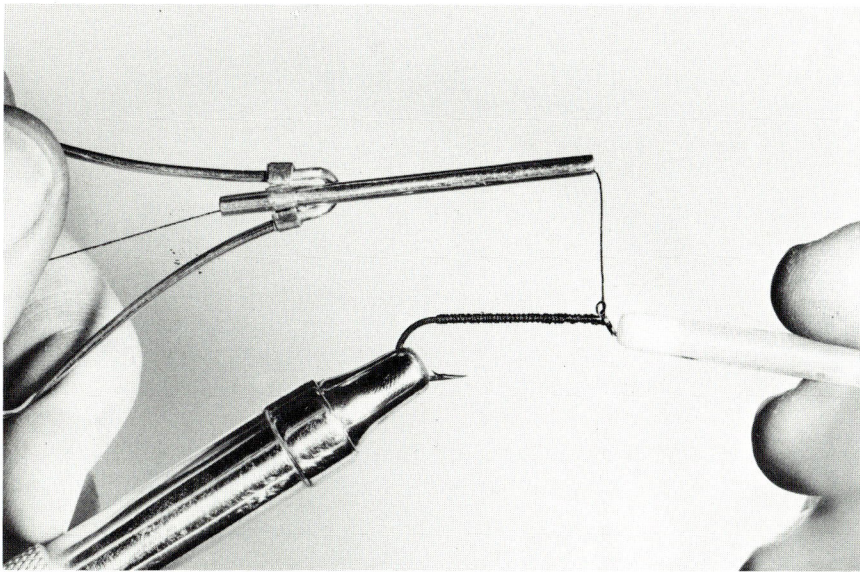

6.4
Slip the knot out by pulling the
bobbin-holder away. Remove
the half-hitch tool and tighten.

Method 7

THE FINAL KNOT

7.1
Hold the silk in the spring
retainer and place the nose hook
under the silk close to the fly-
hook.

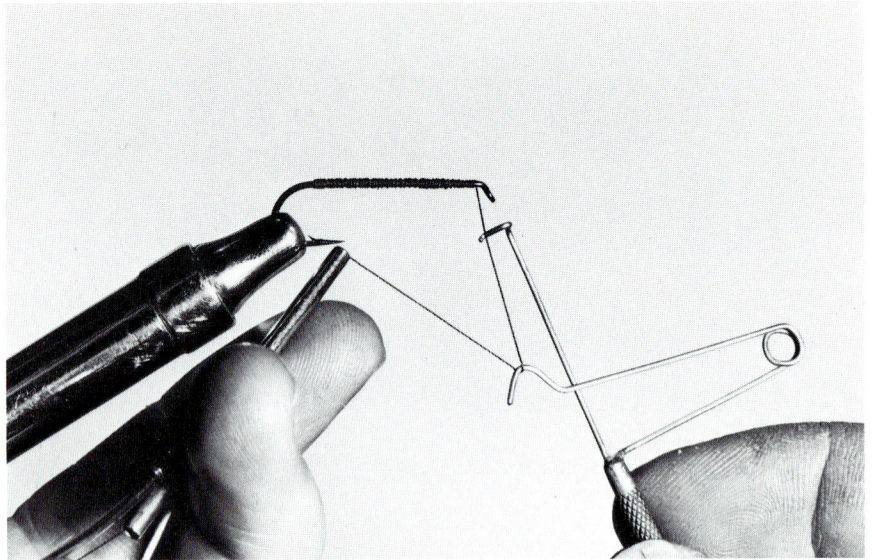

7.2
Maintaining a uniform tension,
place the bobbin-holder parallel
to the shank. At the same time
apply a turning movement to the
whip-finish tool so as to catch
the silk in the nose hook as it
crosses.

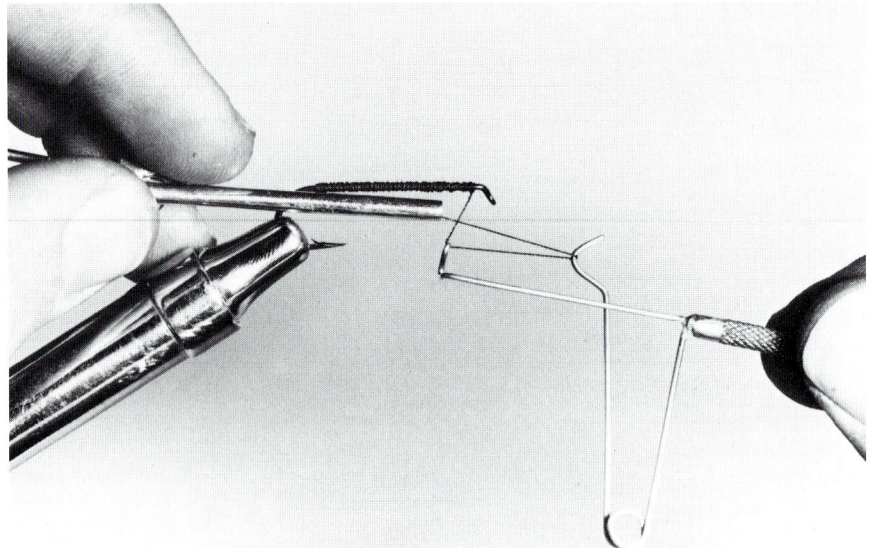

7.3
Rest the bobbin- holder on the
top of the shank. Then, turning
the whip-finish tool in the same
direction, place the guide gently
against the point of attachment.

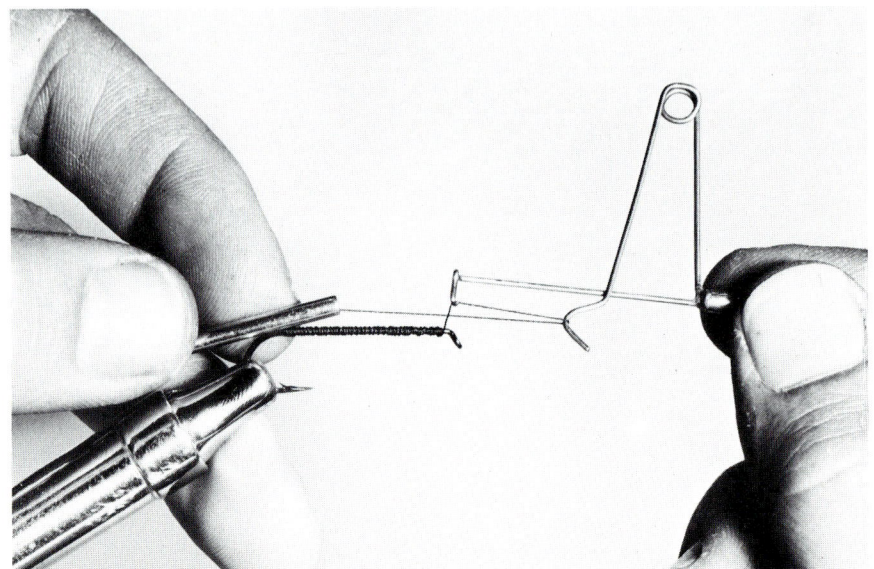

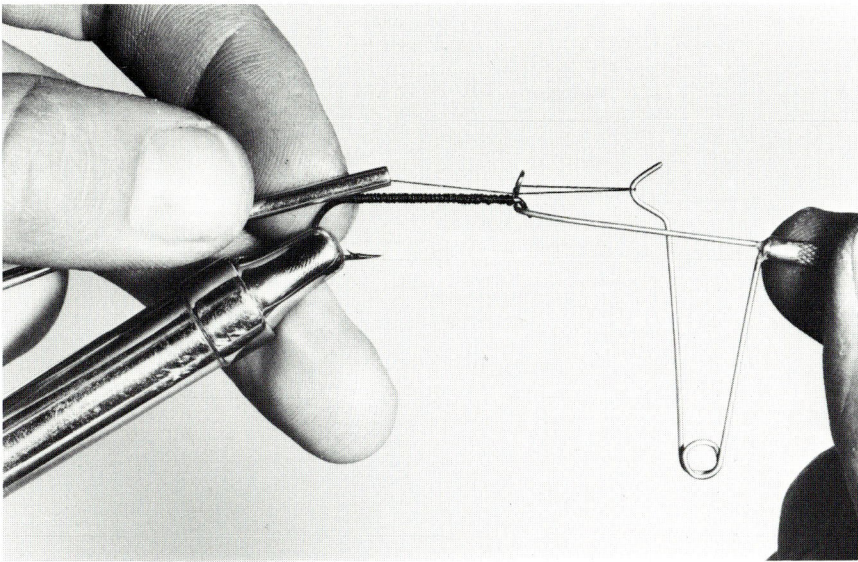

7.4
Make five or six turns with the
silk, fed and aligned by the nose-
hook turning around the same
point.

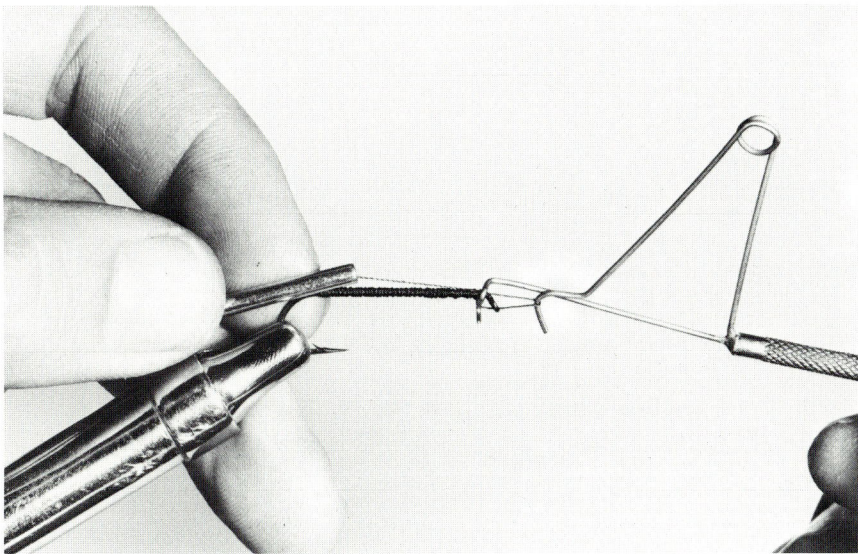

7.5
As the number of turns
increases, the length of silk
between the spring and the nose
decreases. Stop turning when
the spring reaches the position
shown in the illustration.

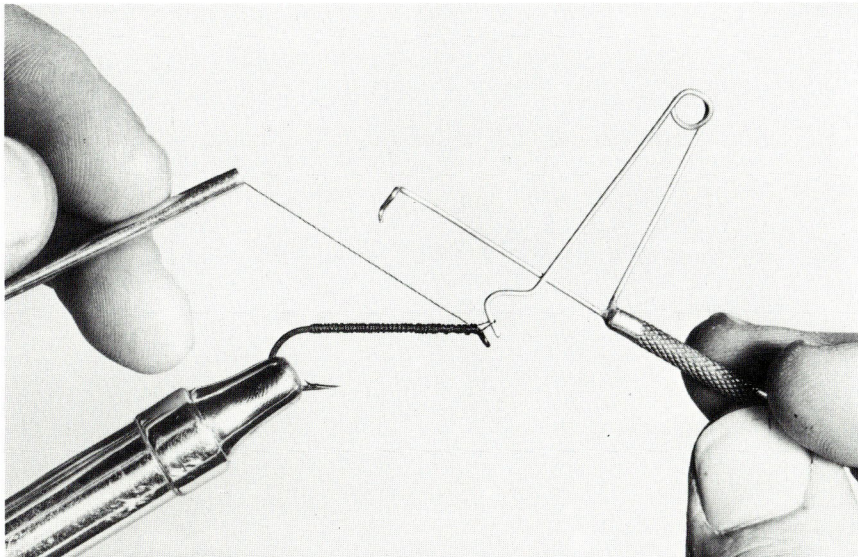

7.6
Disengage the nose and pull the
bobbin-holder away,
maintaining tension on the
whip-finish tool.

7.7
The operation in 7.6 will disengage the spring retainer and all that remains is to cut off the silk at the final knot.

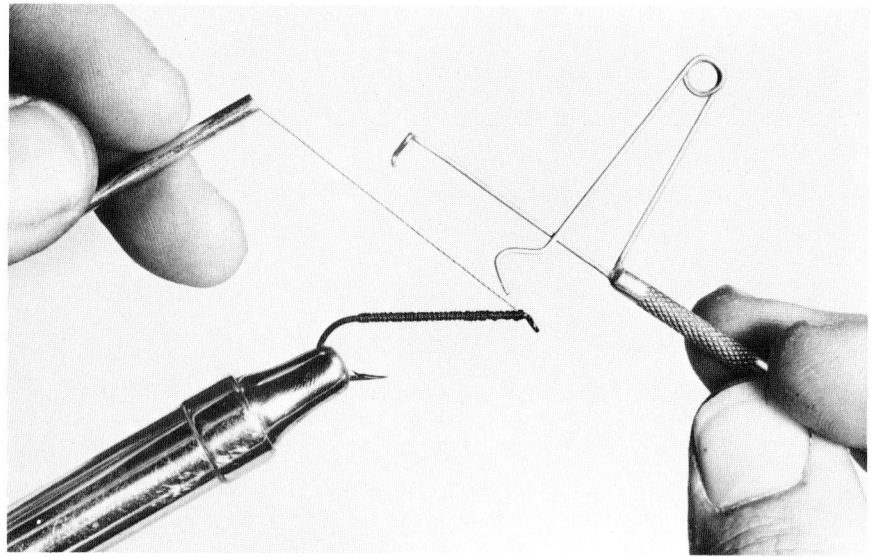

Chapter Four
BUCKTAILS AND STREAMERS

STREAMERS

Streamers are flies designed mainly to imitate small fish. The Americans have subdivided this type of fly into two distinct groups, namely *Streamers*, whose wings are made from feathers, and *Bucktails*, the wings of which are made of hair. Some fly-dressers include neither streamers nor bucktails in the fly category but class them as artificial lures for bait-casting and spinning.

In this chapter we shall use Black Nose Dace and Magog Smelt as examples of the bucktail type; Grey Ghost is used as a sample streamer.

Black Nose Dace

Hook:	Mustad no. 3665A, 9575, 38941 or 79850 nos. 4 to 12
Silk:	Black silk or nylon
Tail:	Red wool (short)
Body:	Flat tinsel, silver
Ribbing:	Optional (oval tinsel, silver)
Wings:	White roebuck (or calf hairs) with black roebuck *or* bear hairs with brown roebuck
Head:	Black
Throat:	Optional (red hackle)
Option:	White eyes with black centre

1

When you have anchored the silk to be used for tying, choose a piece of red wool about 7 cm long and fix it to the shank at the point where the bend starts. If the wool is fine, use double the suggested length. Bind the wool to the shank, winding the silk towards the eye. When you reach the point of attachment, turn back towards the tail and return to the starting point. Cut off the surplus wool and finish with a half-hitch.

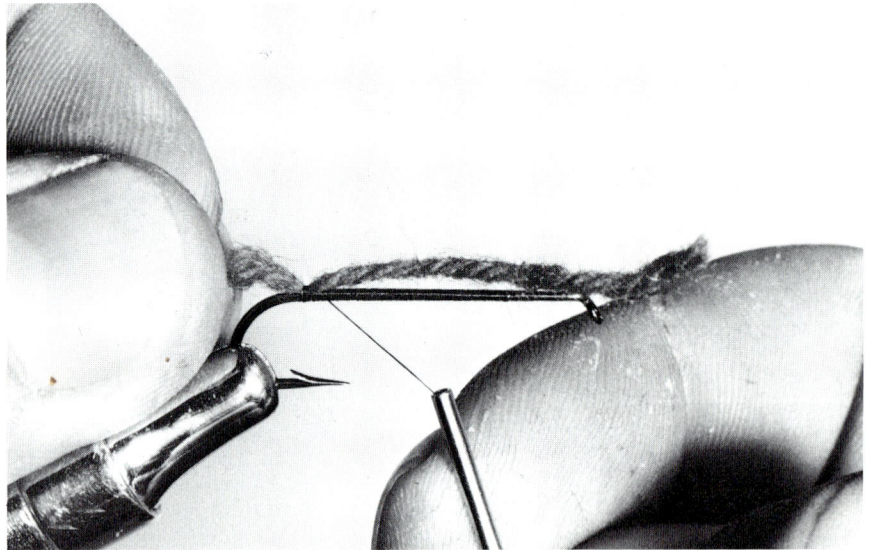

2

Take a piece of silver tinsel 20 cm long in your left hand. Cut the end slantwise and place it alongside the shank at the point of attachment. Fix in position by winding five or six turns of silk.

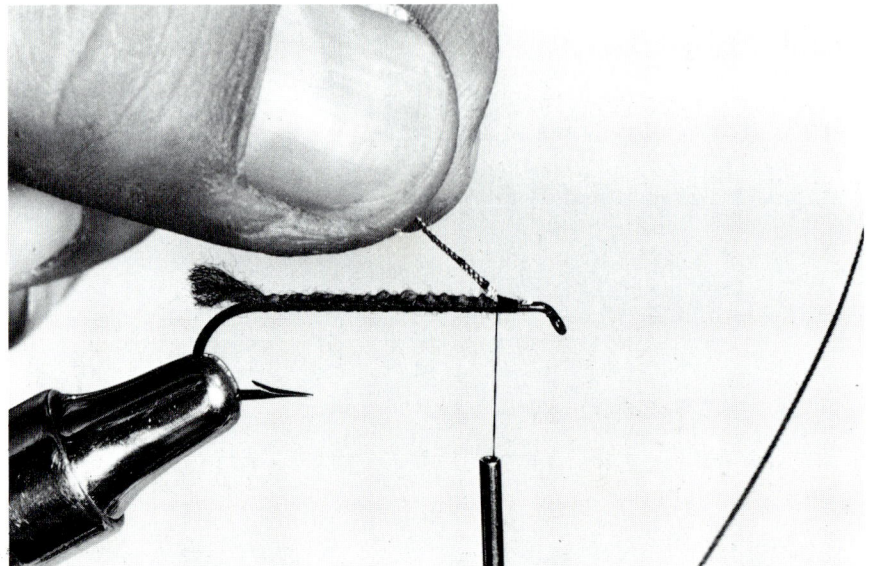

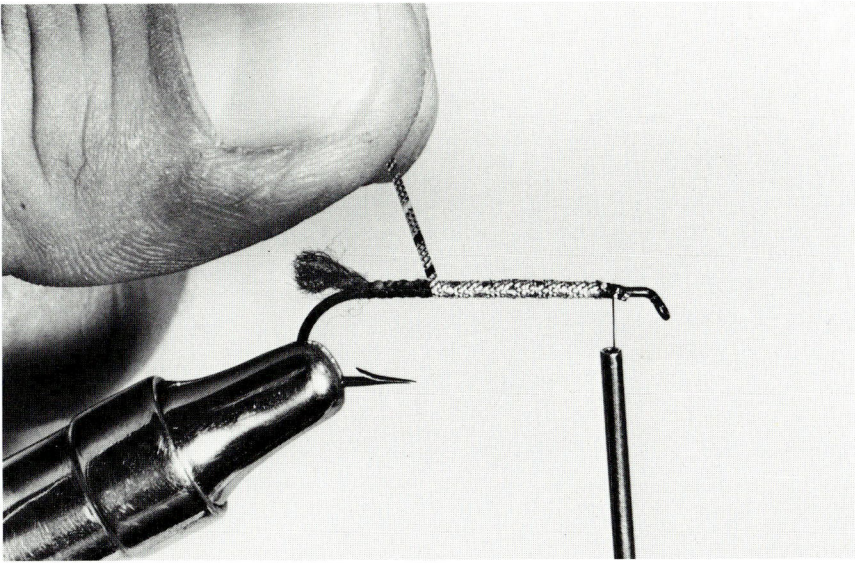

3

Wind the tinsel anti-clockwise, using your right hand for winding. With your left hand, pass the tinsel under the shank. Be careful not to leave any space between the turns, at the same time avoiding any overlapping.

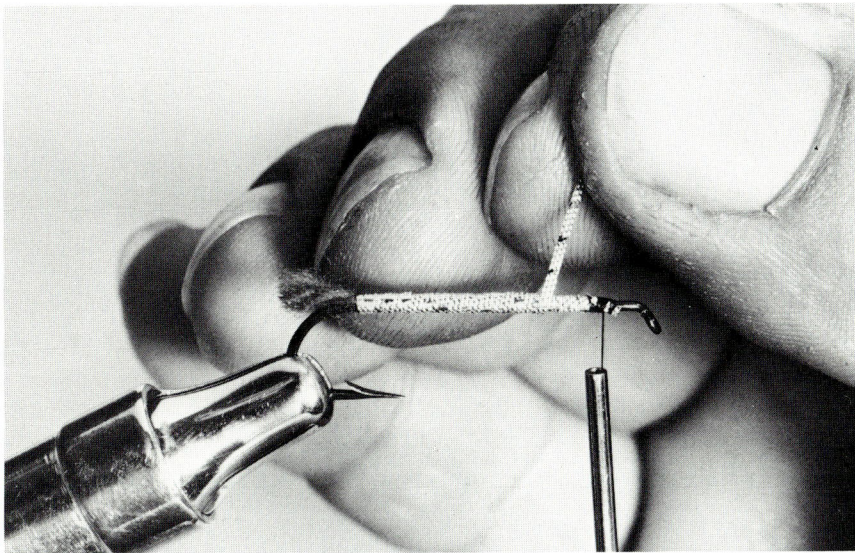

4

When you reach the point where the tail is attached, turn and work towards the front. In this operation as in the preceding one, the turns of tinsel must lie snugly against one another without actually overlapping.

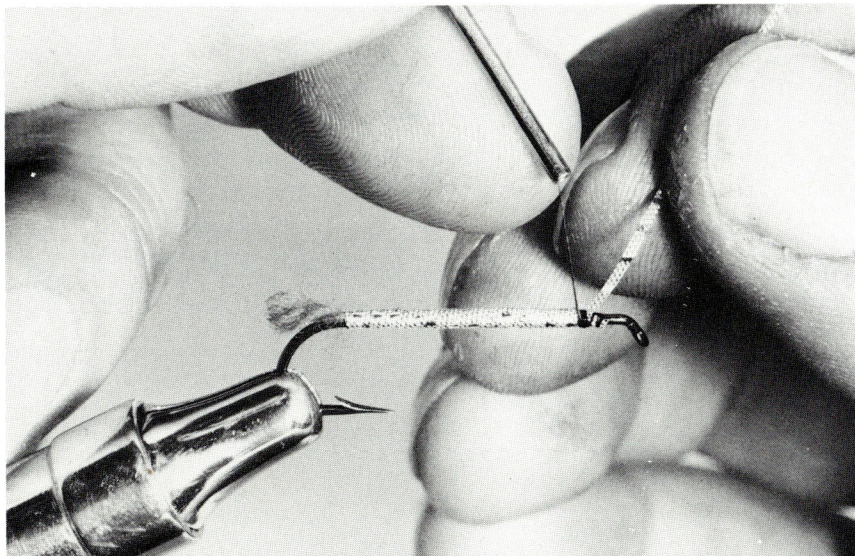

5

With your right hand, hold the tinsel at its starting and finishing point and anchor firmly with three turns of silk. Cut off the surplus tinsel, reinforce with four turns of silk and finish with a half-hitch.

6

Take a pinch of natural white roebuck tail hair and measure the hair against the shank. When in position on the shank, the hair should be one and a third ($1\frac{1}{3}$) times the length of the hook.

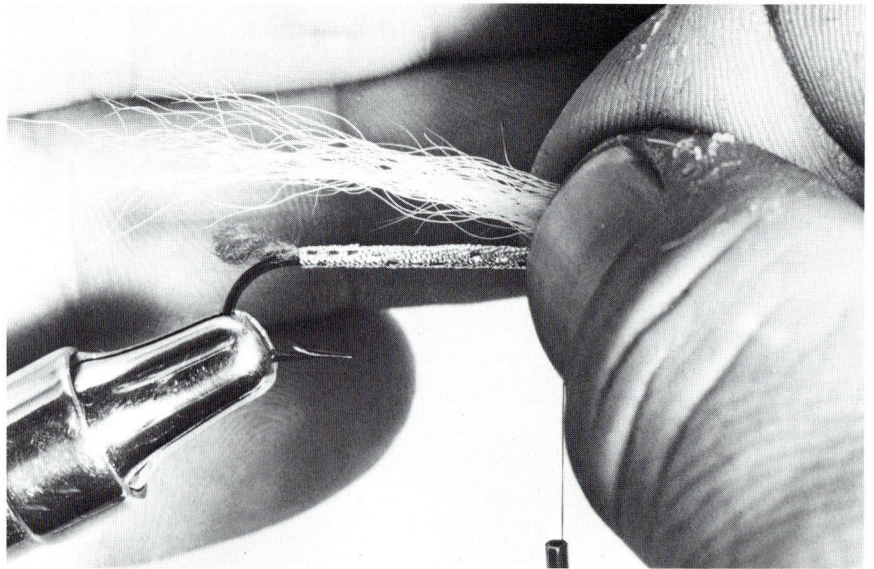

7

Fix the hairs to the main point of attachment by winding four turns of tying silk. Once this operation is complete you can either cut off the surplus hairs slantwise at this point or wait until the tying-in of these hairs (which form the wings of the fly) is complete.

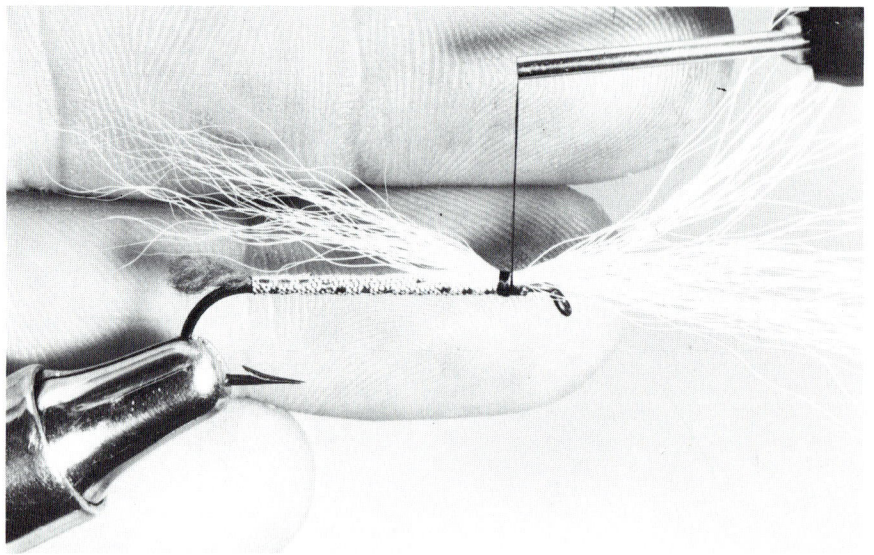

8

Now take a pinch of black hair from the centre of the roebuck tail, selecting the same density as the first. Place the ends of these hairs a little behind and above the others and tie them in the manner already described.

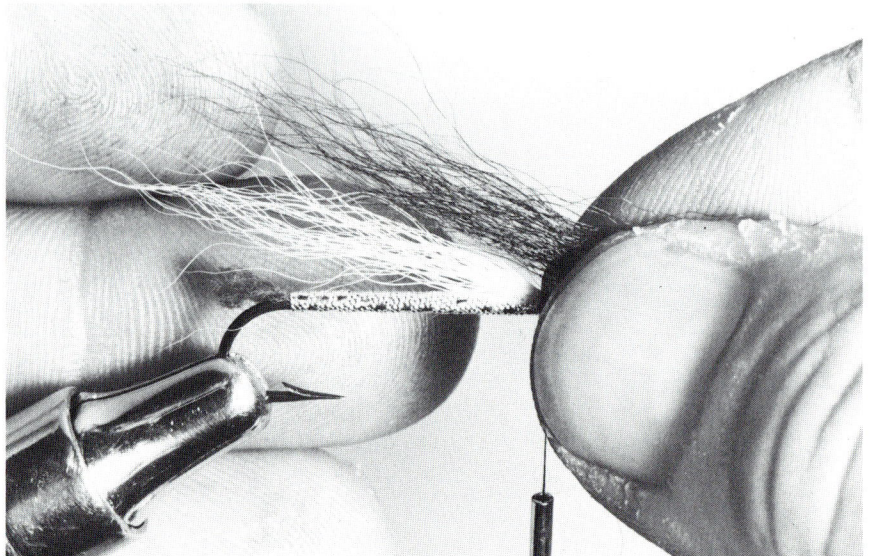

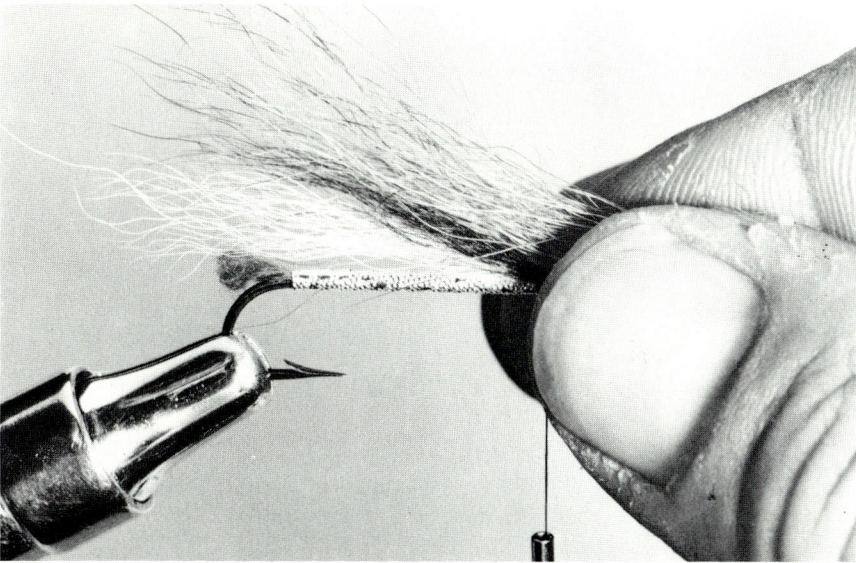

9
Repeat the operation with a
pinch of brown hair taken from
the same tail. These hairs should
be of the same length as the
white ones used in the lower part
of the wing.

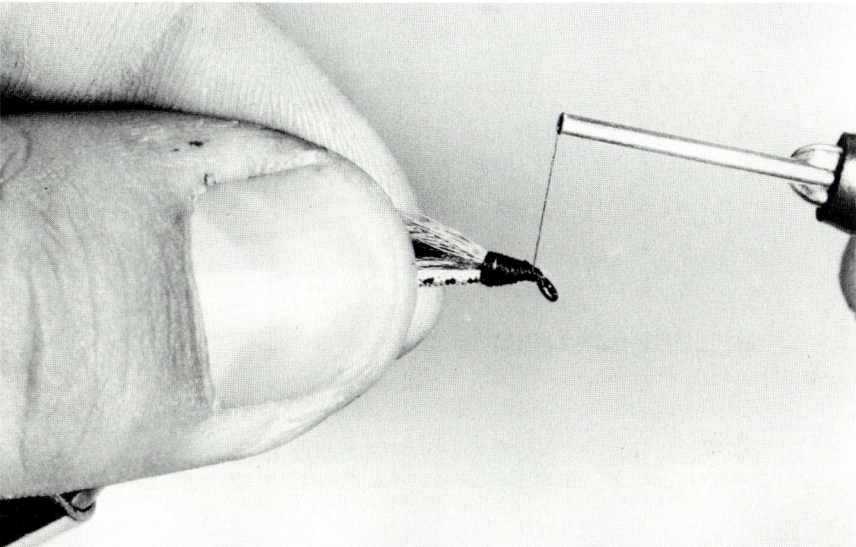

10
Now form a head for your fly by
winding overlying turns of silk.
Finish with a final knot as shown
in Method 7 (pages 40–42).

11
Reinforce the final knot and coat
the head by applying small drops
of varnish with the aid of a
bodkin.

Magog Smelt

Hook:	Mustad no. 79580, 3665A or 9575 nos. 1 to 10
Silk:	Black nylon or silk
Tail:	Fibres from teal flank feathers or striped mallard
Body:	Flat silver tinsel
Wings:	Natural white hair with dyed yellow hair; dyed pale violet hair (all from the tail of roebuck or calf); six or eight peacock tail feather fibres.
Shoulder:	Teal, one flank feather for either side
Head:	Black
Throat:	Red hackle fibres
Option:	Yellow eyes, black centre

1
With the silk tied ready to start, place a portion of teal flank feather along the shank where the bend begins and tie into position.

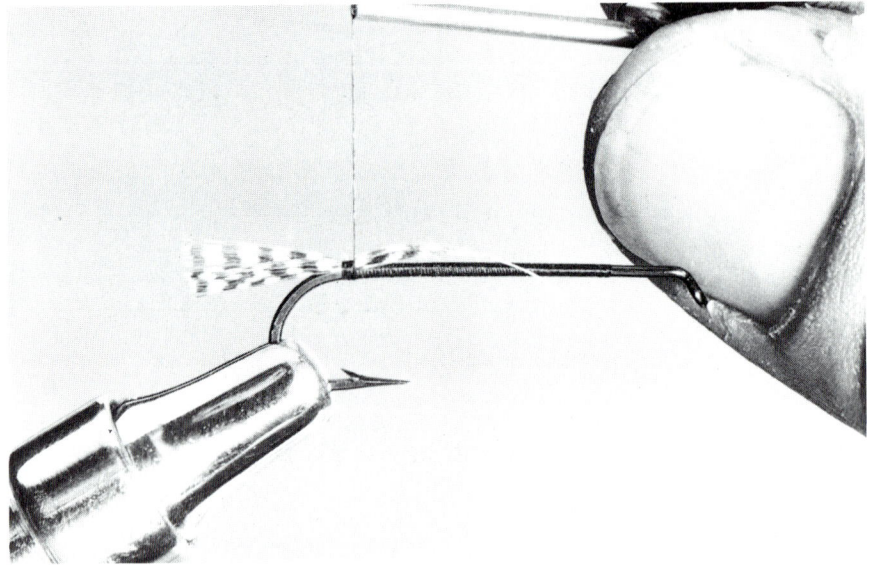

2
Bind the surplus fibres of the feather to the shank, winding the silk towards the eye.

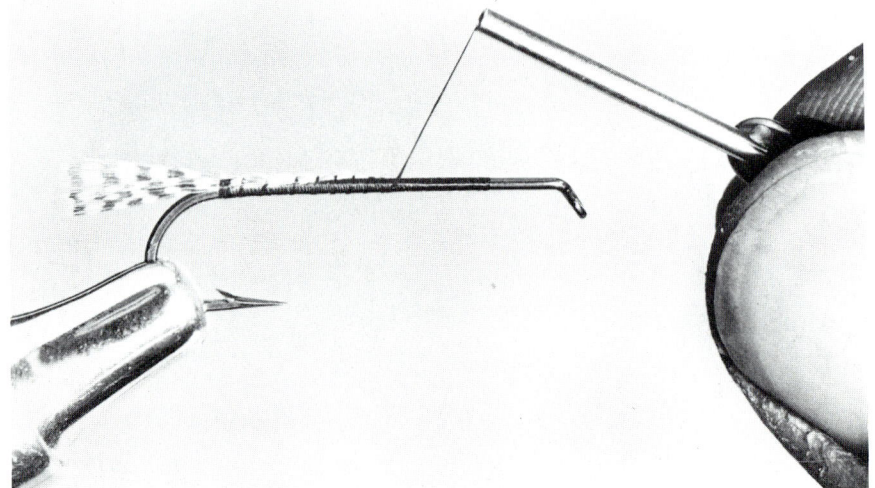

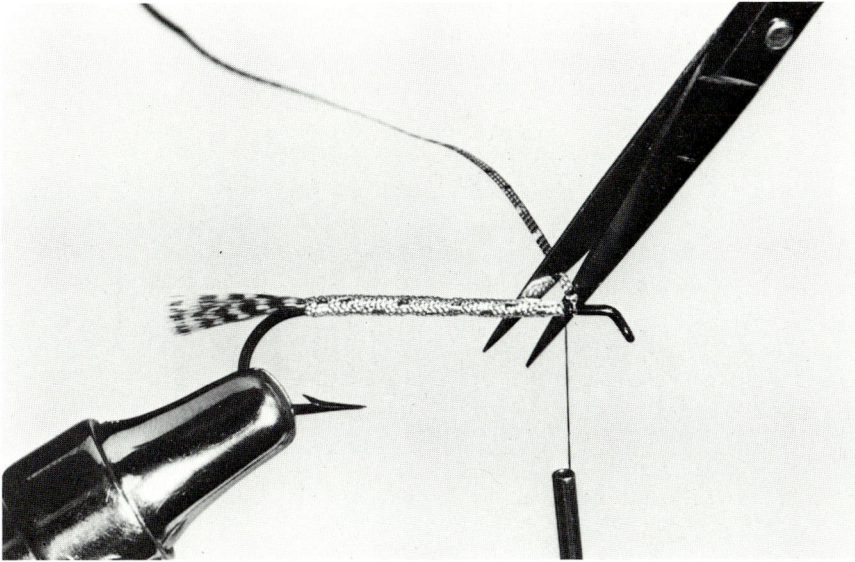

3

When you get back to the point where the silk began, tie in a piece of silver tinsel measuring 20 cm, winding as shown in sections 2, 3, 4 and 5 of the Black Nose Dace (pages 46–7).

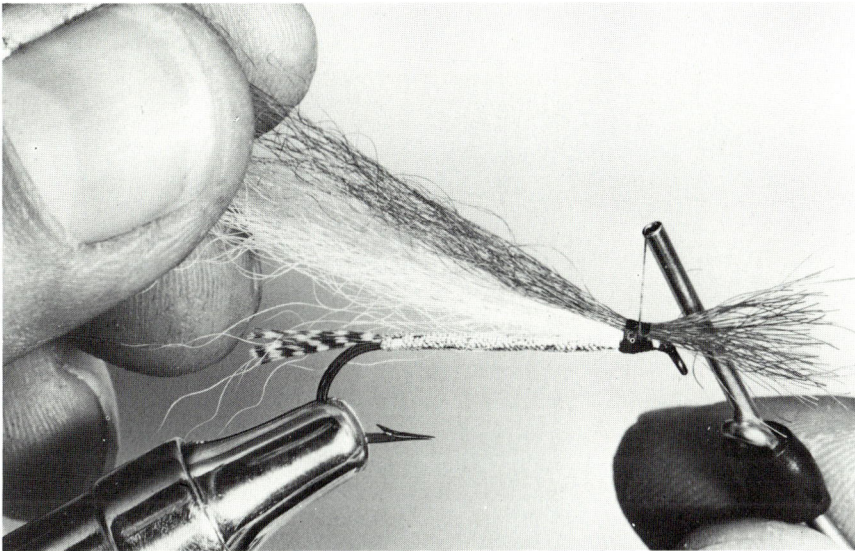

4

Tie the wing of the Magog Smelt securely to the shank. Start with a pinch of black hair then, following the procedure shown in sections 6, 7, 8, 9 and 10 of the Black Nose Dace, tie in the yellow hairs and then the violet ones.

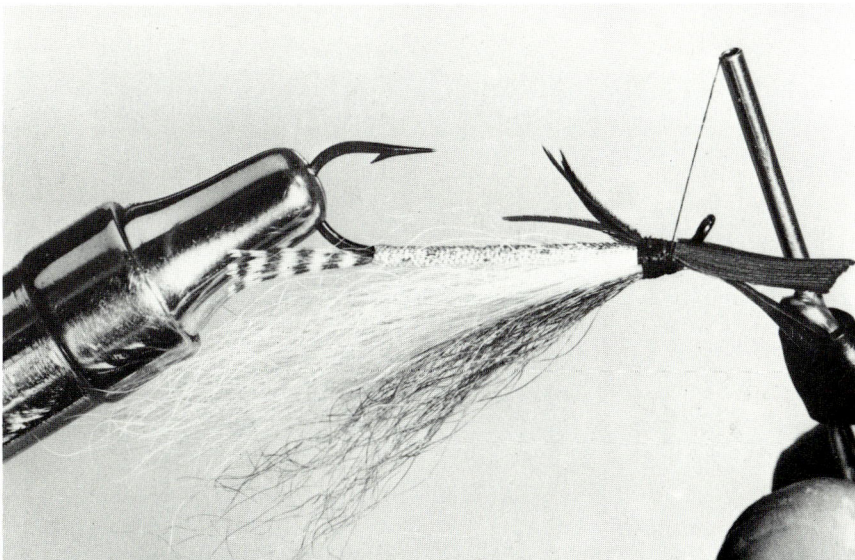

5

Make sure that the wing is firmly fixed by making a half-hitch, then turn the hook over in the vice. Take a piece of red duck feather and place it at the point of attachment. Secure the throat with five or six turns of silk, then finish with a half-hitch and cut off the surplus.

6

Replace the hook in its normal position and select six fibres from a peacock's tail feather. Measure the fibres against the wing and tie them in so that they form a topping for the whole wing.

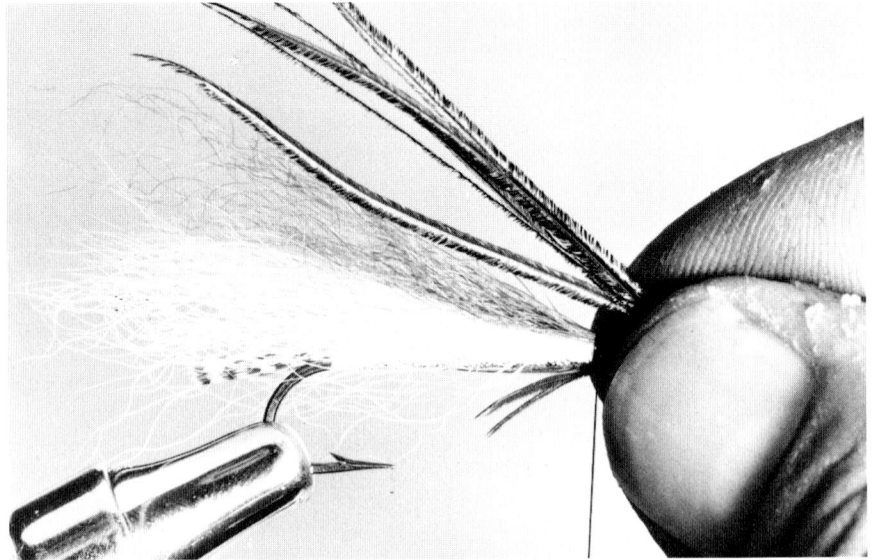

7

Now select two teal flank feathers measuring approximately one third ($\frac{1}{3}$) of the length of the fly. Strip these feathers of their down at the point of attachment. Place the two feathers one on either side of the shoulder, hold them in position with the thumb and index finger of your left hand and tie them in. Cut off the surplus stems, construct the head and varnish.

Grey Ghost

Hook:	Mustad no. 9575 nos. 2 to 12	**Silk:**	Black

Tag: Flat tinsel, silver finish

Body: Orange floss silk

Ribbing: Turns of flat silver tinsel

Wings: Four grey (saddle) hackles

Shoulder: Silver pheasant flank feathers with Jungle cock feathers

Head: Black

Throat: Fibres from peacock-tail feathers, white roebuck tail hairs and fibres from golden pheasant crest feathers

Option: Red collar for the head (original), yellow eyes with black centres if Jungle cock feathers are not available

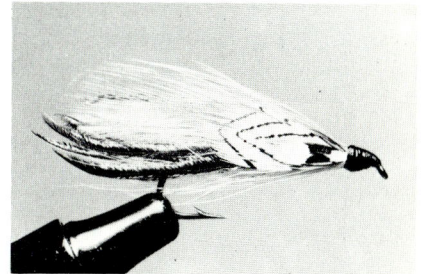

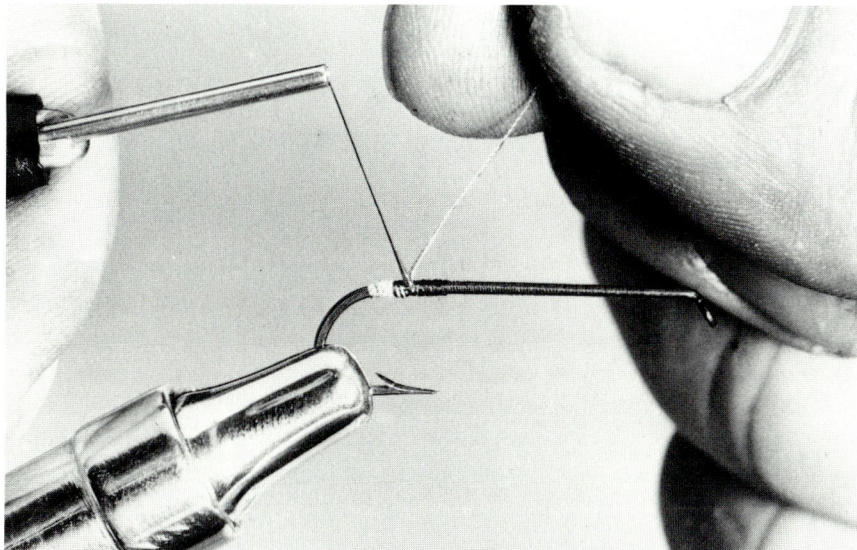

1
Tie on the silk and wind it up to the bend of the hook. At this point tie in a 15 cm length of fine silver tinsel, using five or six turns of tying silk. Form a tag and anchor it at this point.

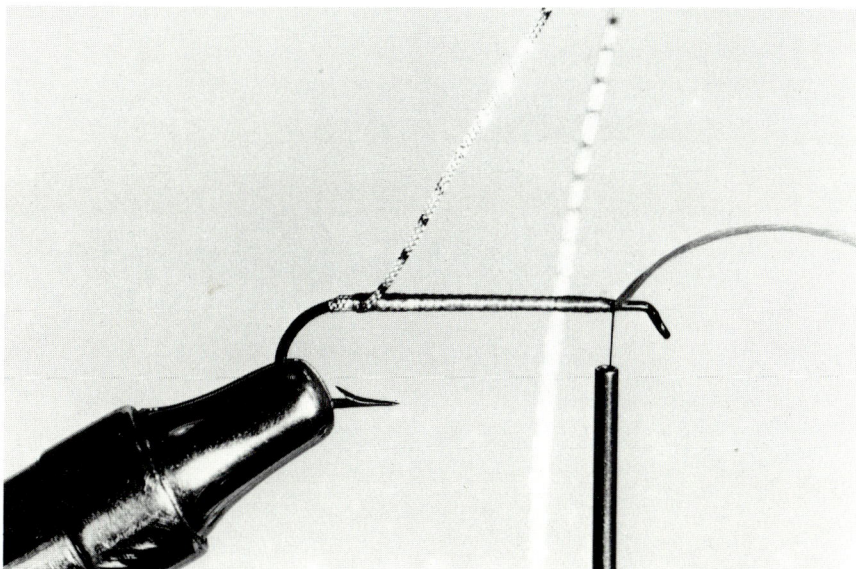

2
Return the silk to the main point of attachment and tie in a piece of floss silk. Using the technique described for forming a tinsel body, cover the shank with floss silk up to the tag. Make a half turn, then come back to the starting point. Tie in the silk, cut off the surplus and finish with a half-hitch.

3

Take the tinsel and wind it
round the floss silk body,
keeping the turns tight and
equidistant. Work from left to
right and anchor at the main
point of attachment. Cut off the
surplus and finish with a half-
hitch.

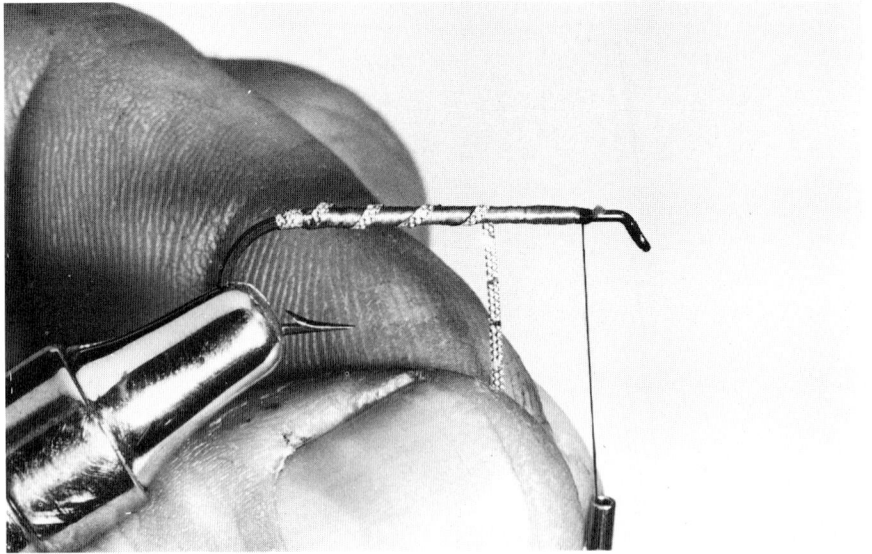

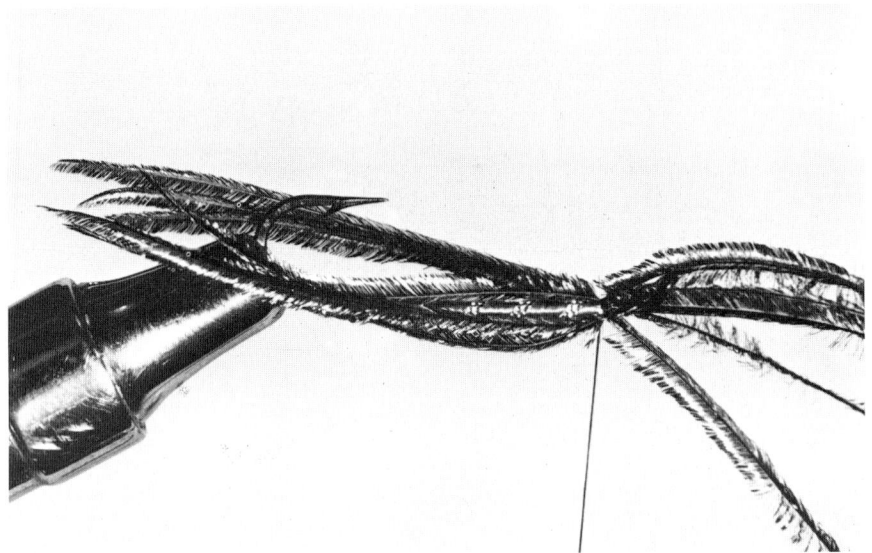

4

Turn the hook upside down in
the jaws of the vice. Select six
feathers from a peacock's tail
feather. Place three of them at
either side of the shank and tie in
firmly at the main point of
attachment. Cut off the surplus
and finish with a half-hitch.

5

Take a pinch of white hair from
a roebuck tail. Measure them
against the peacock fibres and tie
them in at the main point of
attachment. Cut the surplus
hairs off slantwise and finish
with a half-hitch.

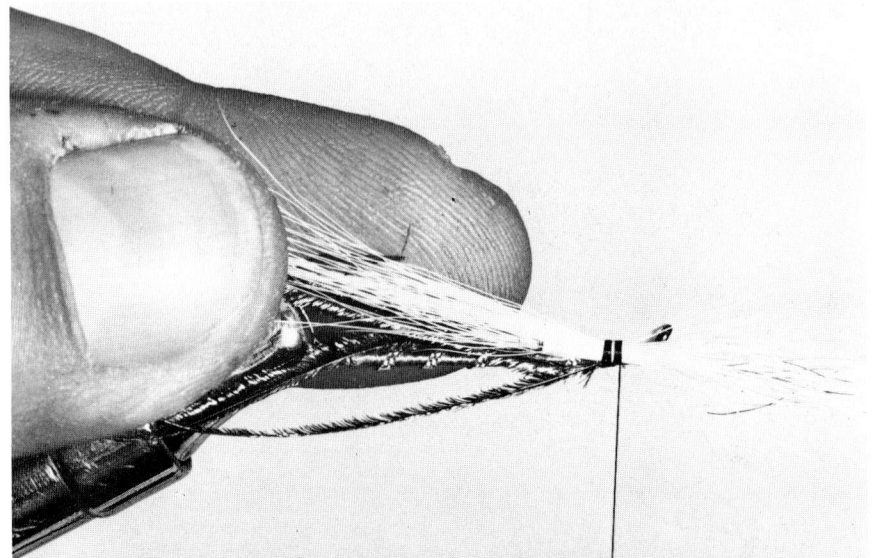

6

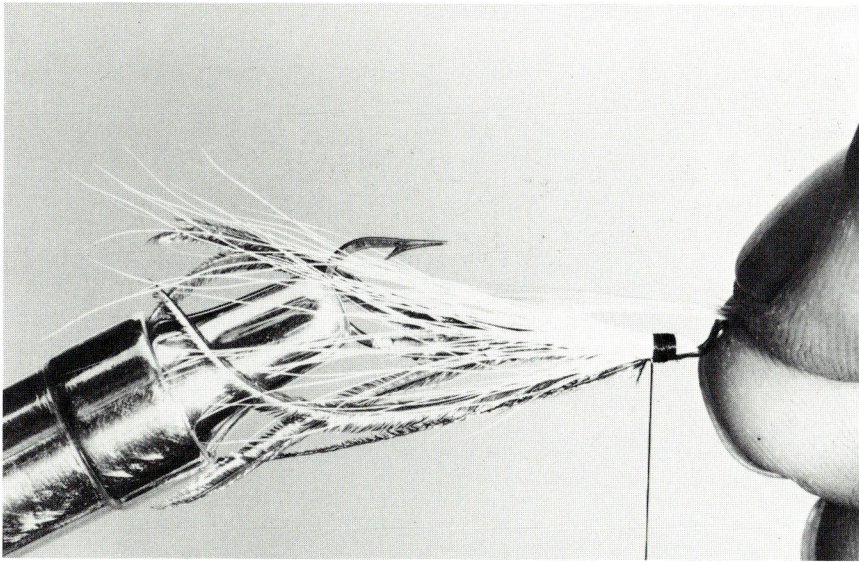

Take a stem, complete with fibres, from the crest of a golden pheasant. Once in place, the stem should be half the length of the shank. Tie this feather in firmly, cut off the surplus and finish with a half-hitch.

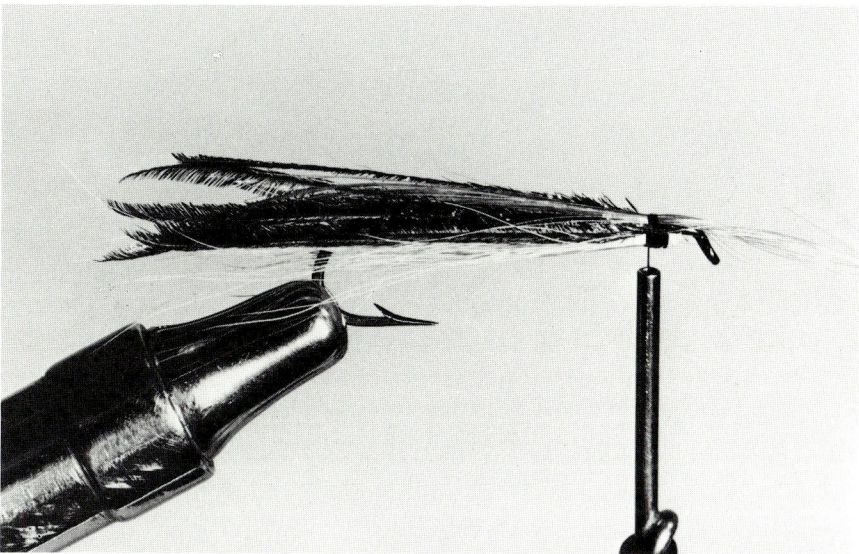

7

Turn the hook over again, thus returning it to its normal position. Take a second crest feather and tie it in at the point of attachment so that it covers the shank of the hook completely. Tie in firmly, cut off the surplus and finish with a half-hitch.

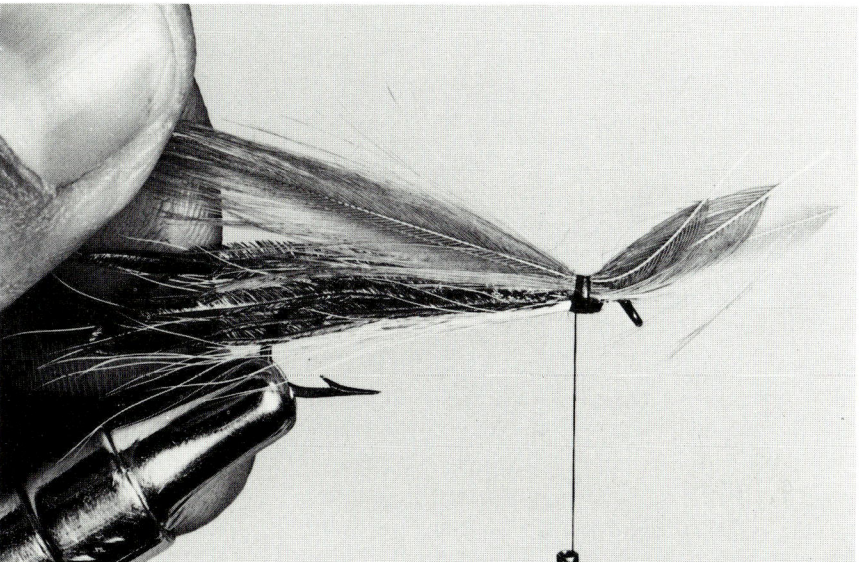

8

Now select four grey saddle hackles, divide them into two pairs and place the hackles against one another with their insides facing. Place them on top of the shank and tie them in firmly at the main point of attachment.

9

Cut off the surplus hackle stems slantwise. Bind them with several turns of silk, making sure that the wings lie straight along the shank, and finish with a half-hitch.

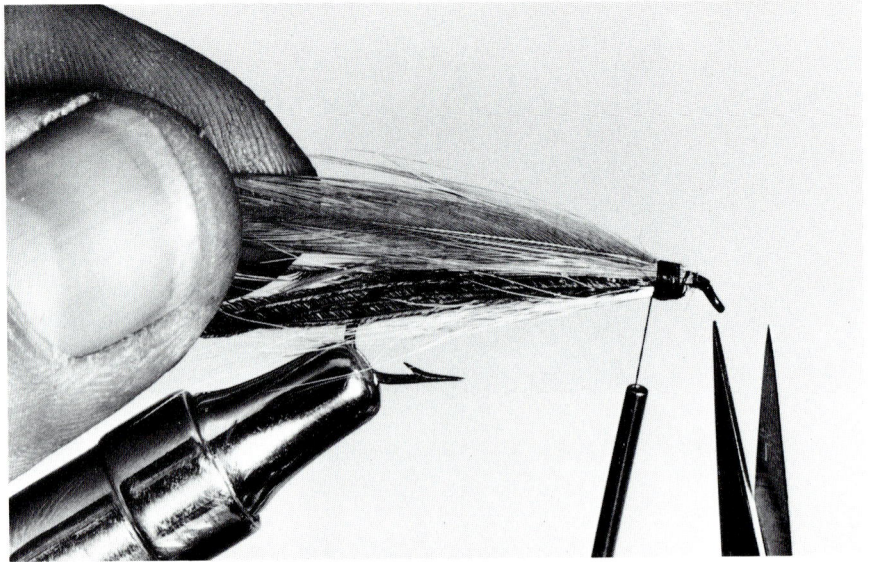

10

Select two feathers from the neck of a silver pheasant. Strip the stems of down and position them at the shoulder of the fly, one on either side. Tie them in firmly, cut off the surplus stems and finish with a half-hitch.

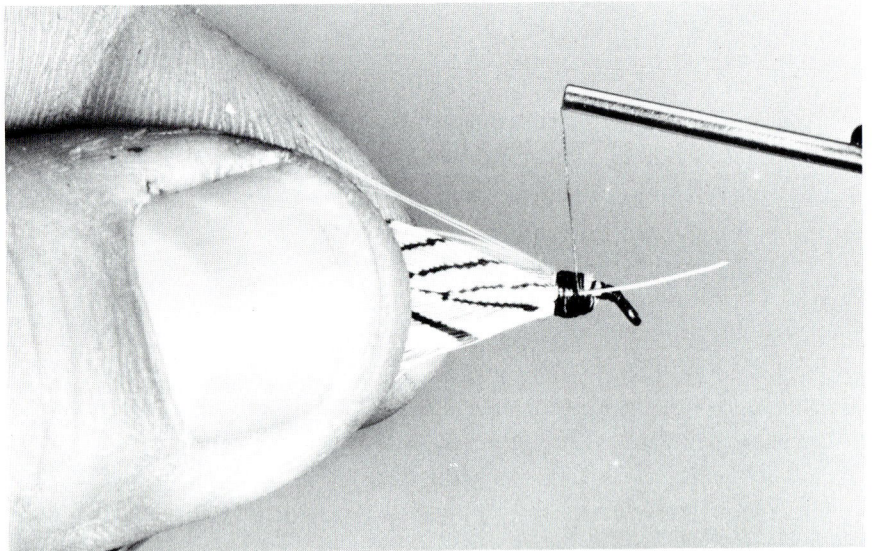

11

Select two Jungle cock(eye) feathers, place one on each shoulder to act as eyes and tie in firmly. Cut off any surplus, construct the head and tie the final knot. Apply varnish and allow to dry.

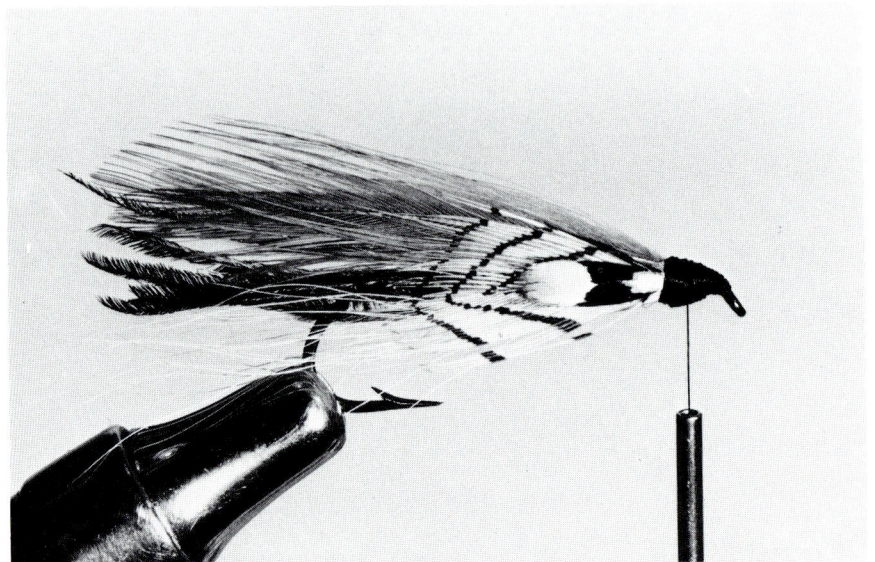

Chapter Five

WET FLIES

WET FLIES

If you examine a typical wet fly closely you will see that it bears a fair resemblance to a mayfly or a sedge fly rising to the surface of the water without its nymph-case and with its wings folded on its back. This rise lasts only for a short time, but the use of the wet fly at this stage produces good results, despite the fact that its name suggests the opposite of this normal process in the evolution of insects.

In this chapter we shall go through the stages in the dressing of two flies – the Dark Hendrickson and the Coachman. The former represents no insect in particular and the latter the mayfly Subvaria.

Dark Hendrickson

Hook:	Mustad no. 9671 nos. 10 to 14
Silk:	Black silk or nylon
Tail:	Grey-blue hackle fibres or fibres from the flank feather of a crested duck
Body:	Grey musk rat fur
Throat:	Grey-blue hen hackle fibres
Wings:	Fibres from flank feather of a crested duck

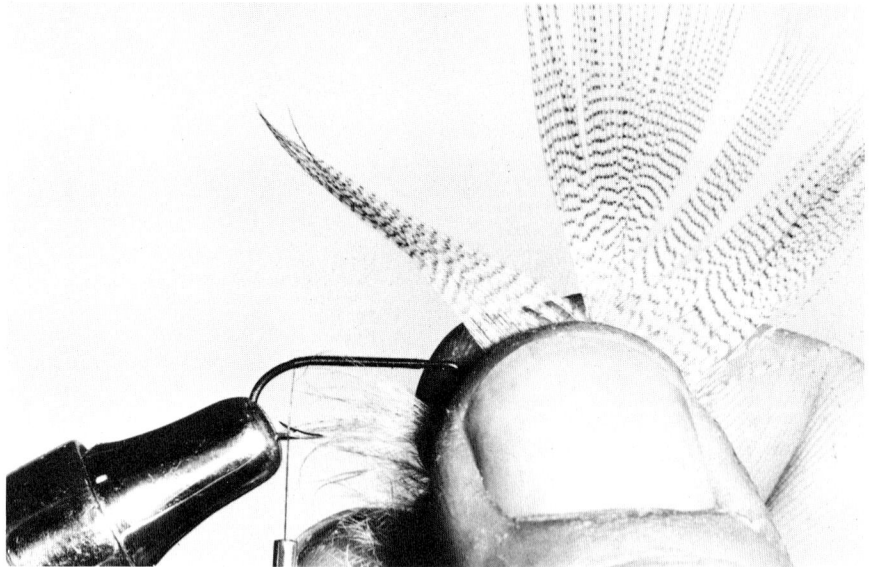

1
Anchor the tying silk 3 mm from the eye and wind it along as far as the beginning of the bend. Select a crested duck flank feather and remove one or two fibres from it.

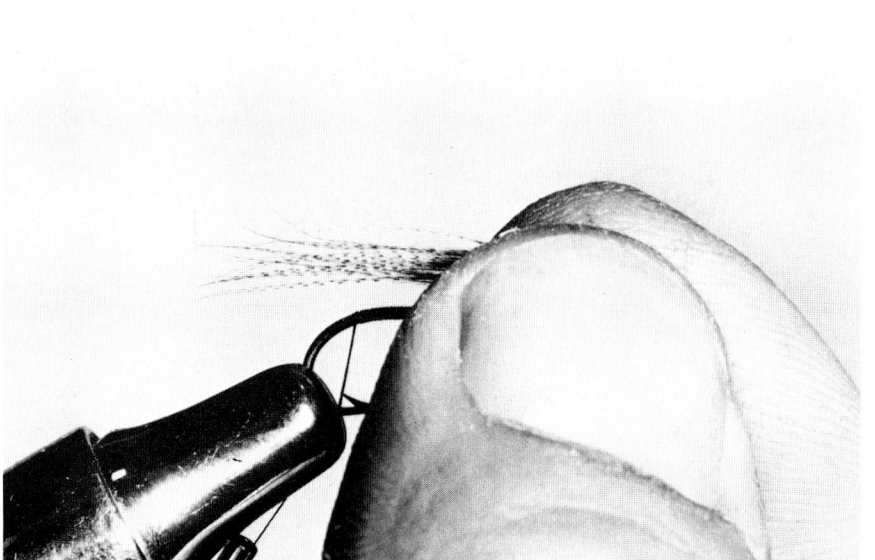

2
Cut the chosen fibres and anchor them at the point where the bend begins. Once in position, the length of the tail should be equal to the length of the shank.

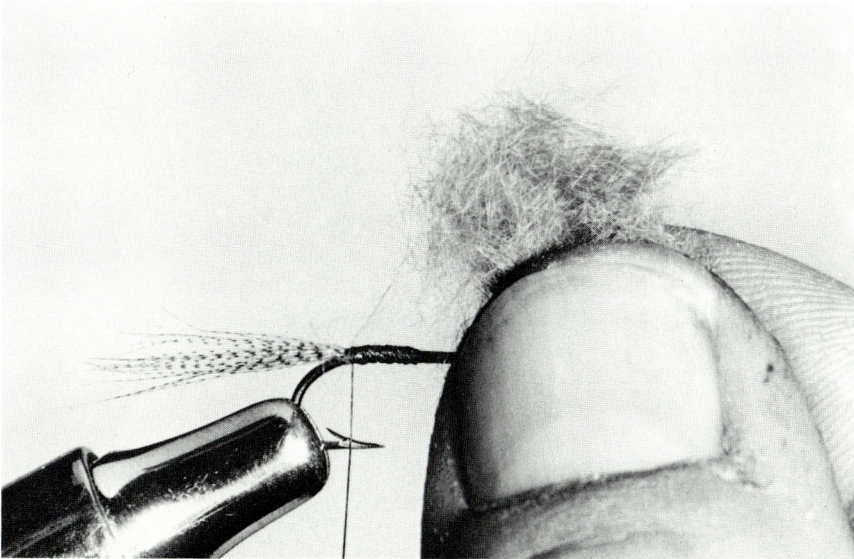

3
Using your all-purpose scissors,
take a pinch of musk rat fur.
Remove the stiff hairs and comb
out the soft ones.

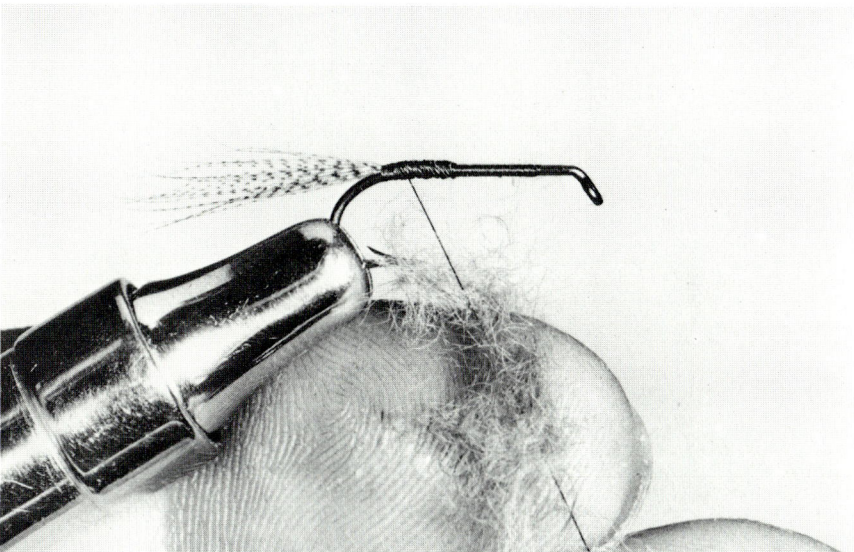

4
Wax the silk, then place little
pinches of soft fur on it.

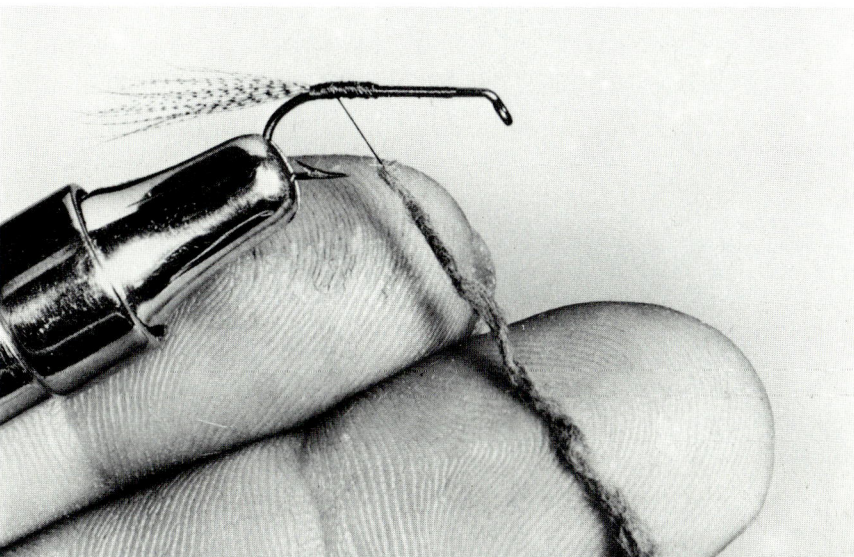

5
Roll fur and silk between your
fingers. Apply pressure and
continue rolling in one direction
only until you have produced
5 cm of fly body material.

6

Wind the prepared material on
to the hook shank in tight turns.
Anchor firmly at the main point
of attachment and finish with a
half-hitch. A tufted body,
though aesthetically preferable,
does not seem to have any more
attraction for the fish.

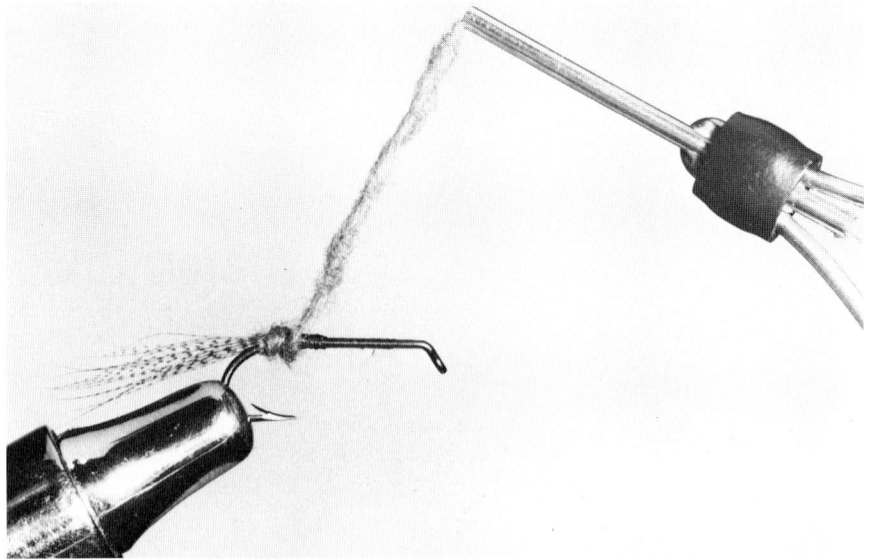

7

Turn the hook upside down in
the jaws of the vice. Take a
pinch of grey hackle fibres to use
as legs and anchor these fibres so
that they cover the tip of the
barb. Cut off the surplus and
finish with a half-hitch.

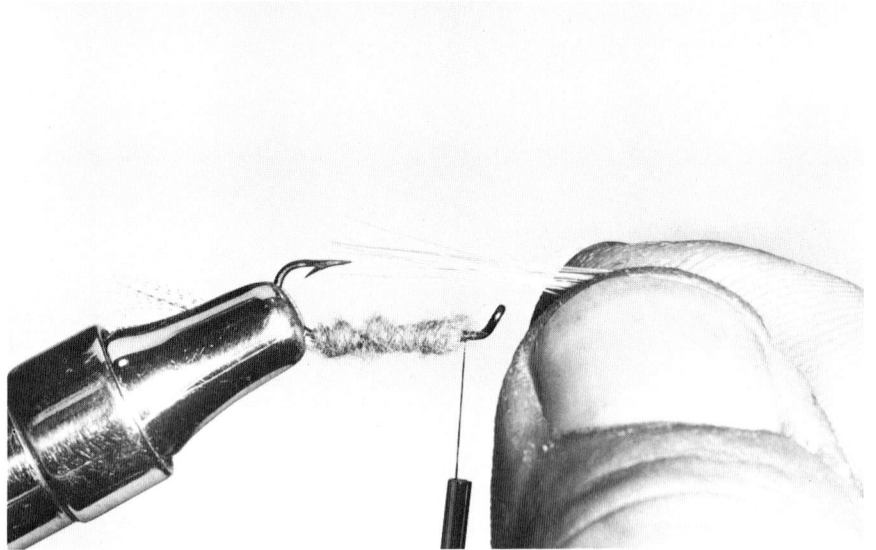

8

Replace the hook in its original
position. Cut about 1.3 cm of
fibres from the same crested
duck flank feather used in
operation 1. Wind these fibres
into a tight tuft.

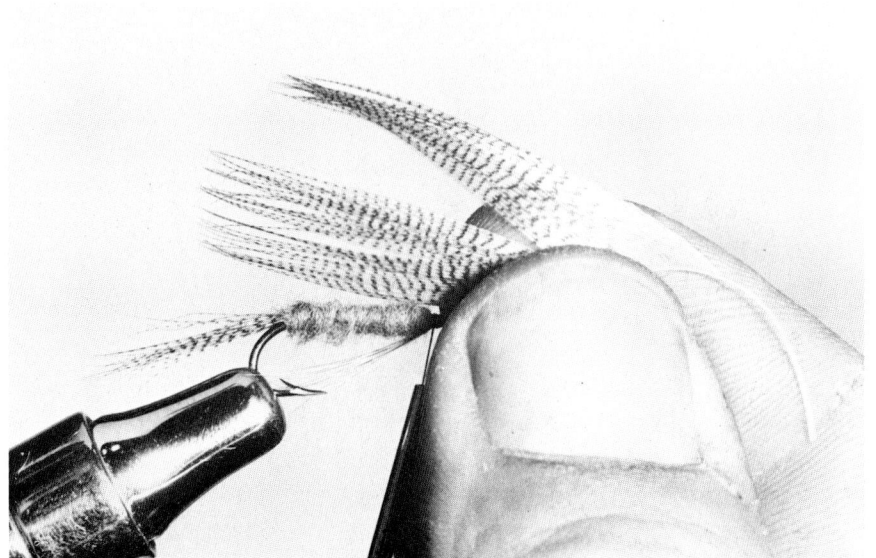

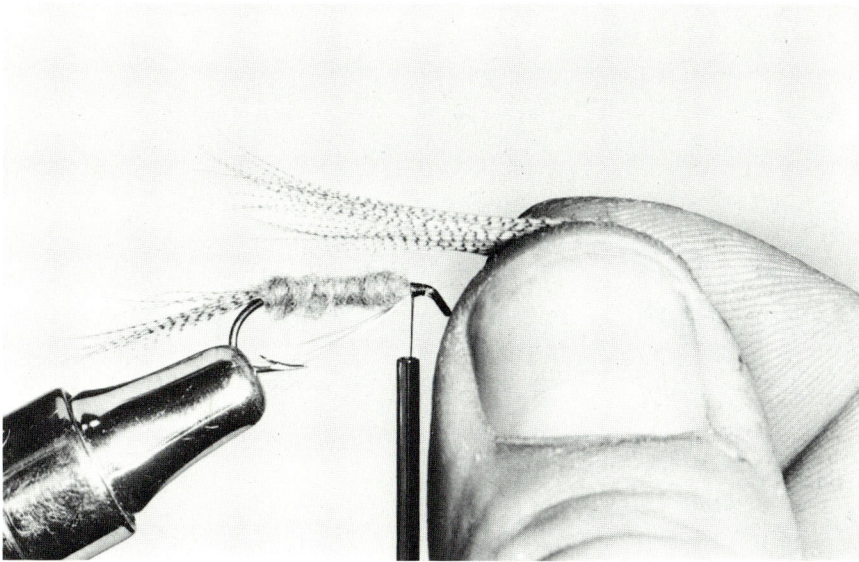

9
Measure the tuft of fibres against the fly and tie them in at the main point of attachment, so that the tips of the fibres reach halfway along the tail.

10
Anchor firmly, cut off the surplus and construct the head. Proceed to tie final knot and varnish.

11

Coachman

Hook:	Mustad no. 9671 nos. 12 to 14
Silk:	Black silk or nylon
Tag:	Optional. Flat gold tinsel
Tail:	None
Throat:	Brown hackle fibres
Wings:	Section of white feathers, duck or goose

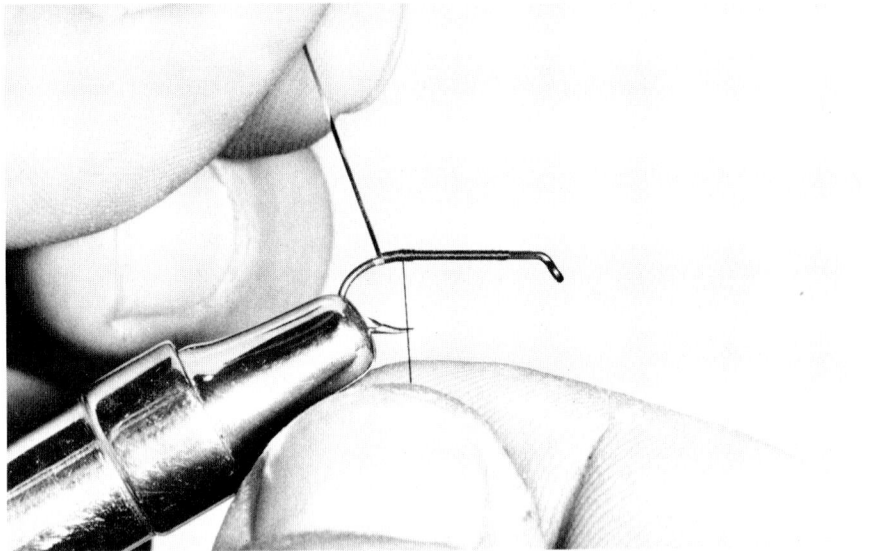

1
Anchor the tying silk 3 mm from the eye and wind it along to the bend of the hook. At this point, tie in a 10 cm length of fine flat gold tinsel.

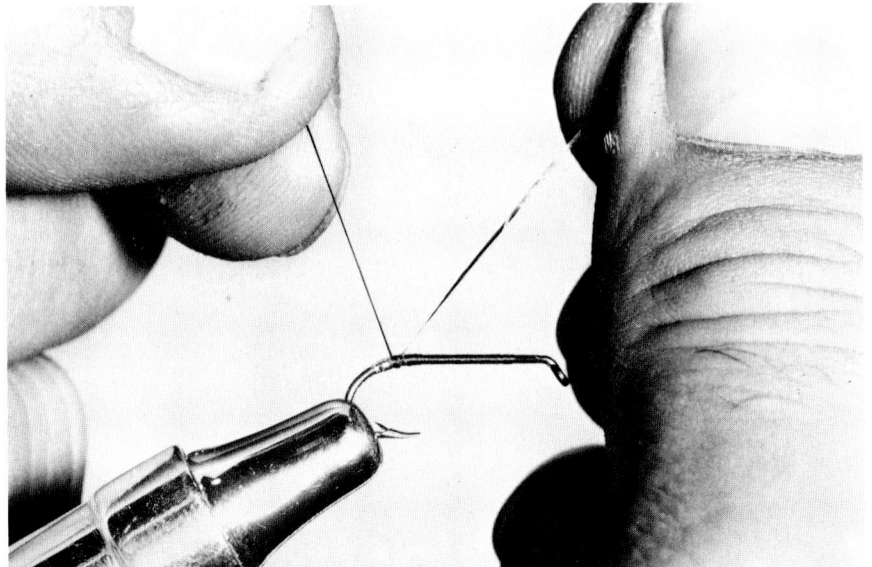

2
Wind the tinsel towards the left for about 2 mm. Return to the right, making tight turns, and tie off at the starting point. Reinforce with a few turns of silk and cut off the surplus tinsel.

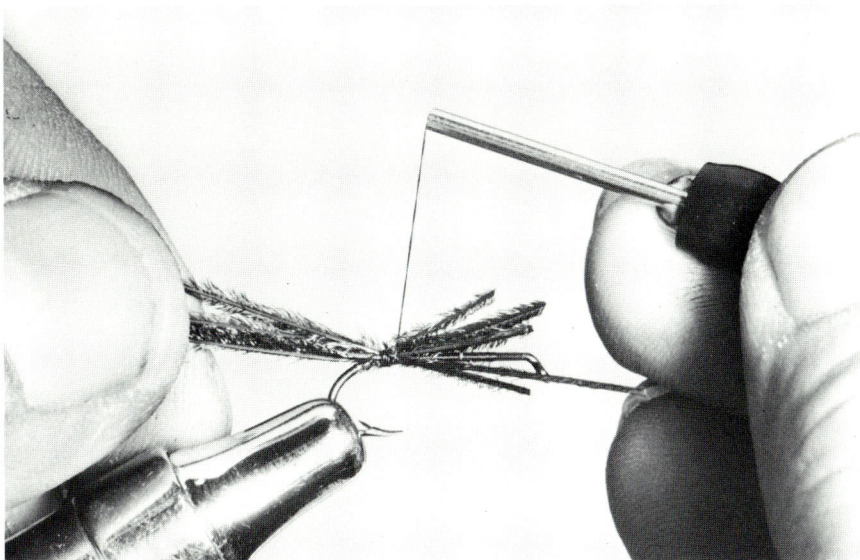

3
Select six fibres taken from the base of the eye of a peacock's tail feather. Tie them in firmly under the shank and cut off the surplus.

4
Make a loop about 20 cm long and reinforce with a whip-finish. Return the silk to the main point of attachment.

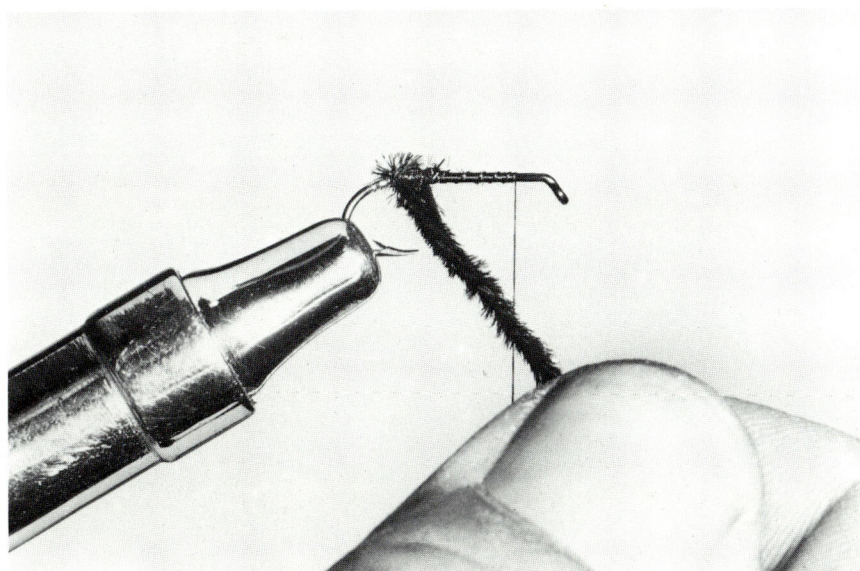

5
Bring the strands together and place them in the loop. Spinning the strands and the silk between your thumb and index finger will form a firm twist of peacock fibres. Form the body, anchor it at the starting point, cut off the surplus and finish with a half-hitch.

6

Turn the half-finished hook
upside down in the vice. Select
about a dozen large brown
hackle fibres and place them at
the point of attachment in such a
way that their tips touch the
barb. Cut off the surplus and
reinforce with a half-hitch.

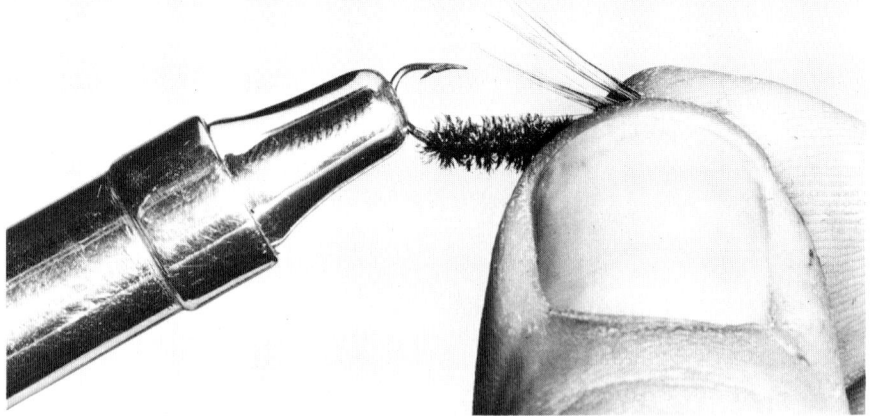

7

Put the fly back in its original
position and select two white
duck feathers. With the aid of
scissors take out two identical
sections, each 5 mm wide.

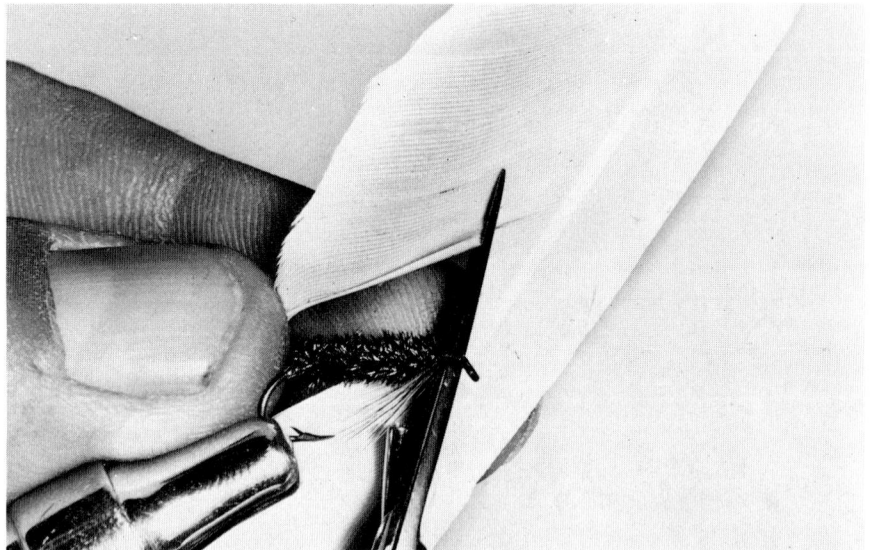

8

Place the sections together so
that their tips are equal, with the
shiny or concave surfaces on the
inside, facing one another.

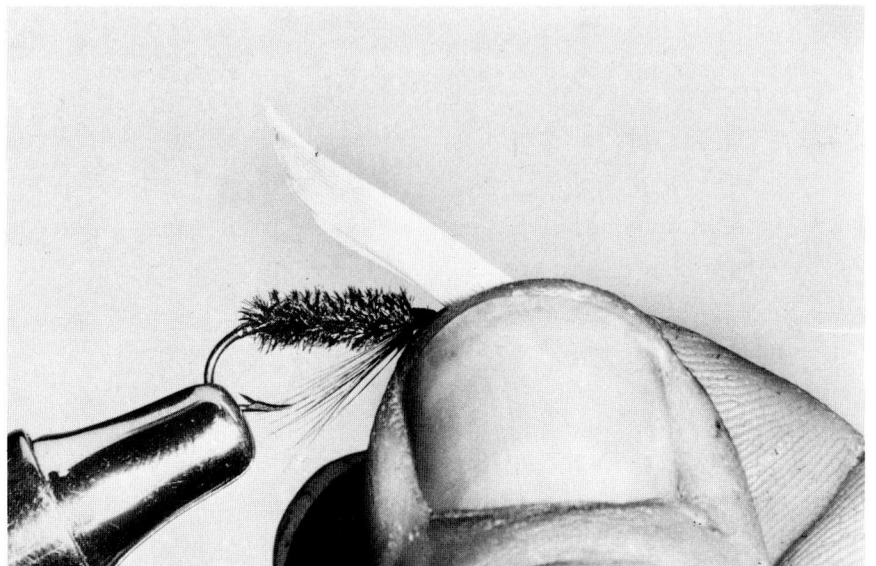

9
Position the wings so that they stretch the whole length of the hook. Hold the whole fly between the thumb and index finger of your left hand and anchor at the point of attachment.

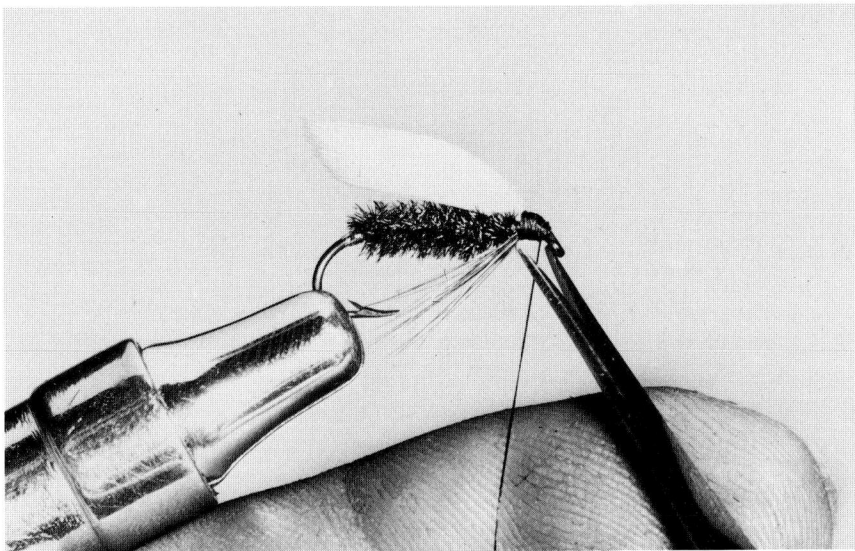

10
Cut off the surplus, reinforce by constructing the head, tie the final knot, cut the silk, varnish and set aside to dry.

Chapter Six

NYMPHS

NYMPHS

Artificial nymphs are dressed to imitate ephemera, diptera, etc. In the second stage of their metamorphosis – the stage between the larva and image – these insects represent an important part of the trout's diet.

Here are three examples of dressings: the S.J.V. Caddis, Jac's Red Stone and Jac's March Brown.

S.J.V. Caddis

Hook:	Mustad no. 3906 or 3906B nos. 8 to 12
Silk:	Black silk
Body:	White hare's fur
Thorax:	Beaver fur, dyed black
Hackle:	Guinea hen feather

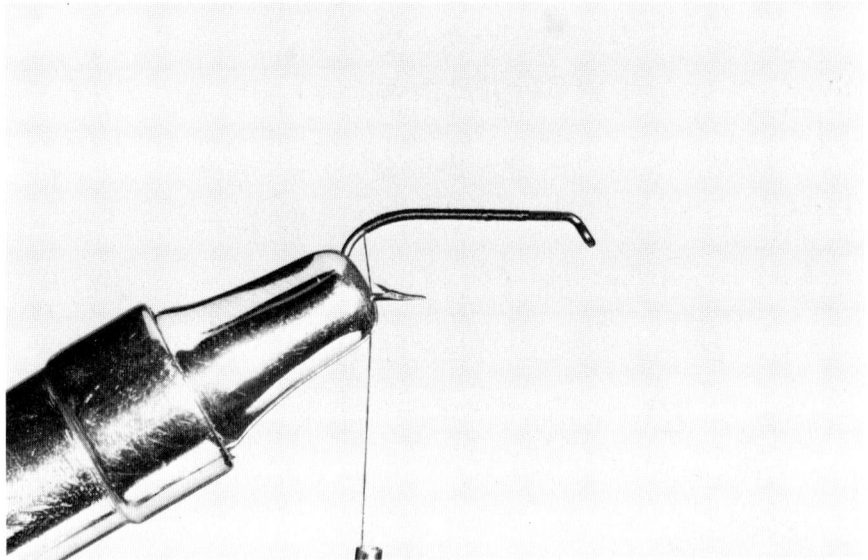

1
Having anchored the tying silk 3 mm from the eye, cover the shank of the hook to a point one quarter of the way round the bend.

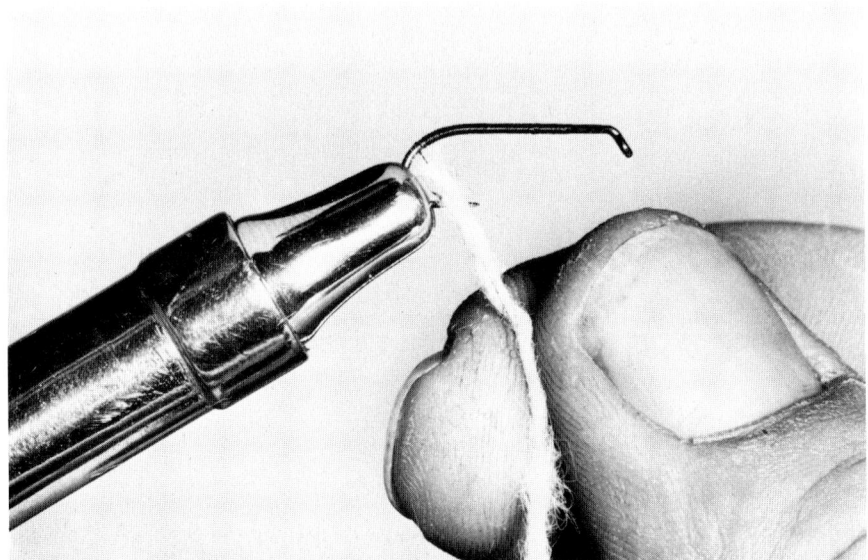

2
Take a pinch of white hair from a hare skin and coat the waxed silk by the method already shown.

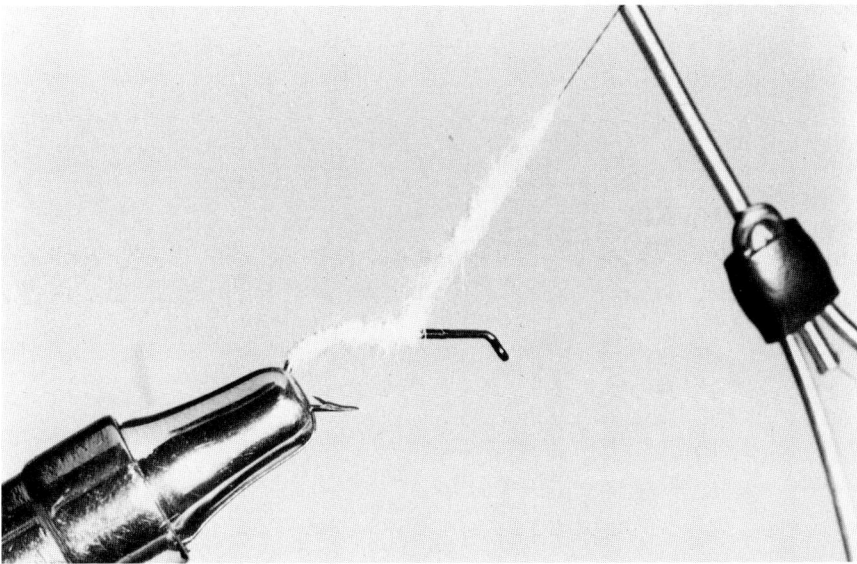

3

Form the body of the fly, making tight turns. Stop 1 mm from the point of attachment and anchor firmly with a half-hitch.

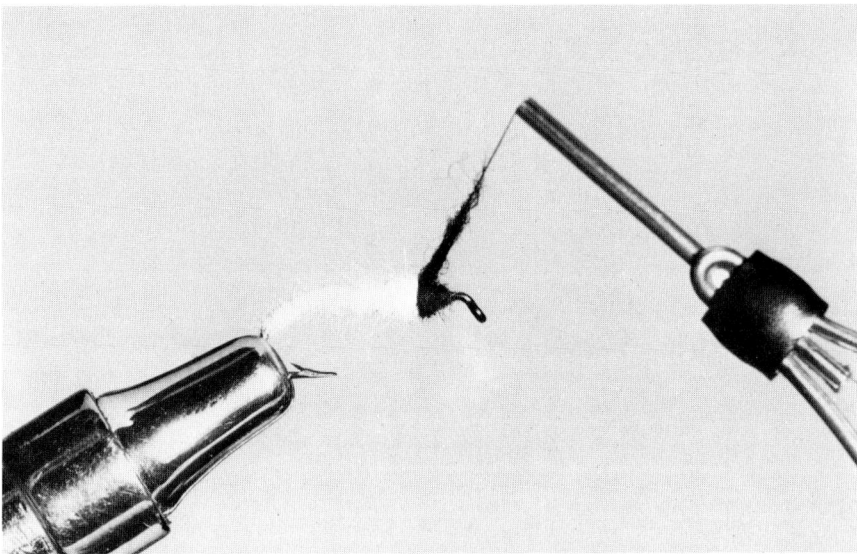

4

Proceed to position the thorax by coating the waxed silk with black fur and winding along 2 mm of the shank. Anchor firmly with a half-hitch.

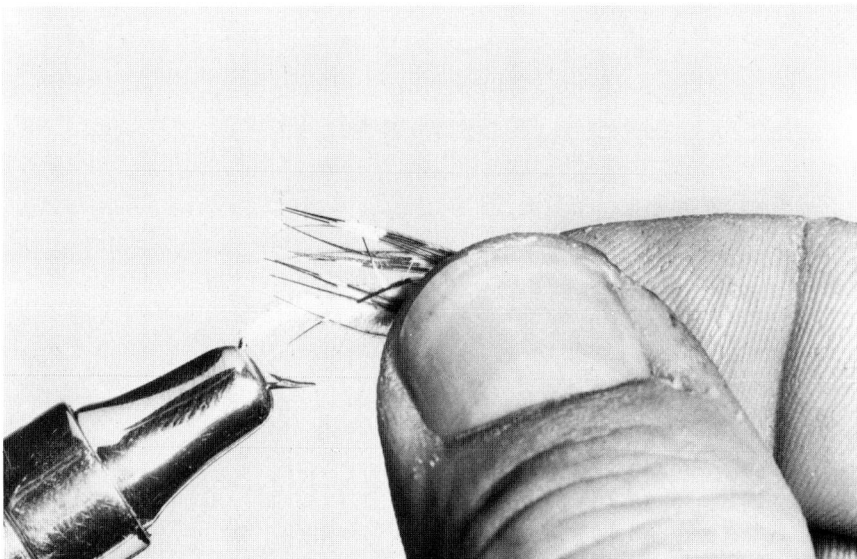

5

Take about a dozen fibres from a Guinea hen feather and place their ends towards the back. Grasp them with your left hand and hold them in place.

6
Make three turns of silk,
allowing the fibres to rotate
freely round the thorax.

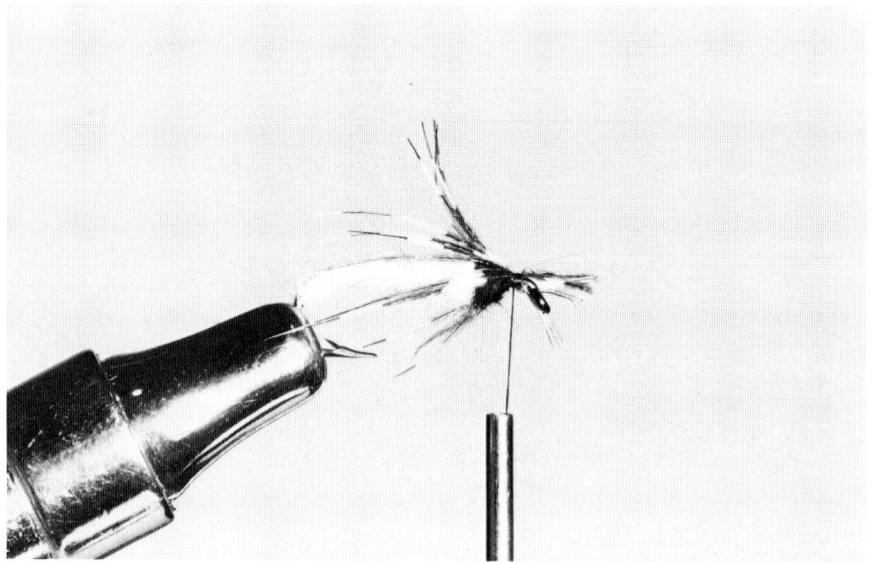

7
Cut off the protruding fibres and
cover the head firmly. Make a
final knot, cut off the silk,
varnish and set aside to dry.

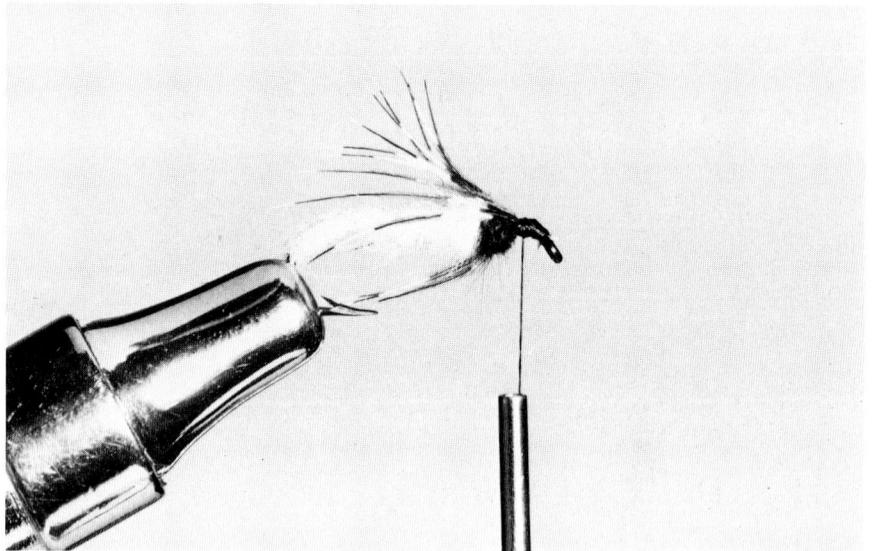

Jac's Red Stone

Hook: Mustad no. 79580 nos. 6 to 12 length 4x

Silk: Black nylon

Tail: Two stripped peacock tail feathers

Wings: Wing-case made from sections of dark turkey feather

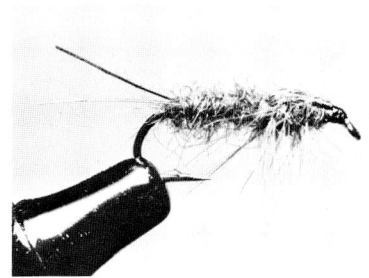

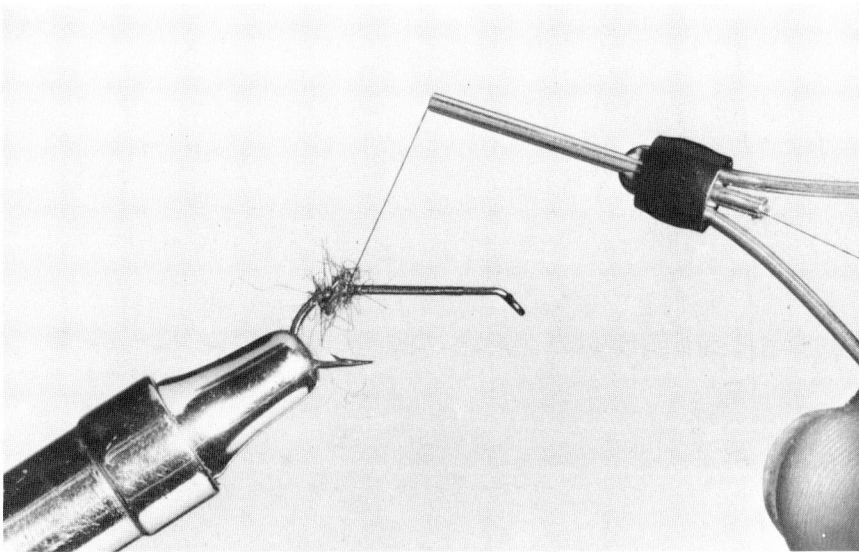

Legs: Brown hackle

1

Anchor the silk about 1 cm from the eye. Cover the shank up to the point where the bend begins. Wax the silk and apply to it a very small pinch of seal hair. Make a bunch and finish with a half-hitch.

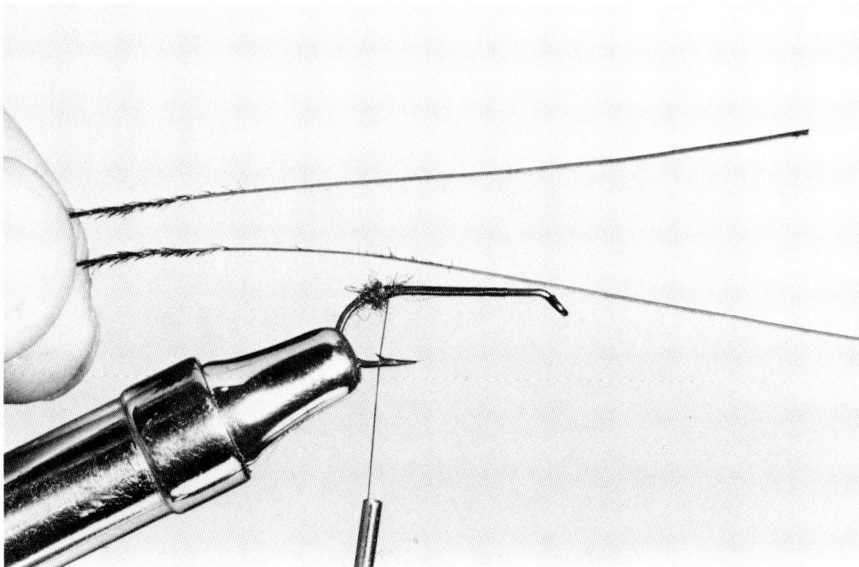

2

Take two fibres from a peacock's tail feather. Strip off the tiny hairs by rubbing the chosen fibres with an eraser.

3

Attach the two stripped fibres firmly, one on either side of the tuft. Work back towards the left, making several turns of silk. As you press the fibres against the pompom of hair in this way, they will divide to form the tail of the nymph.

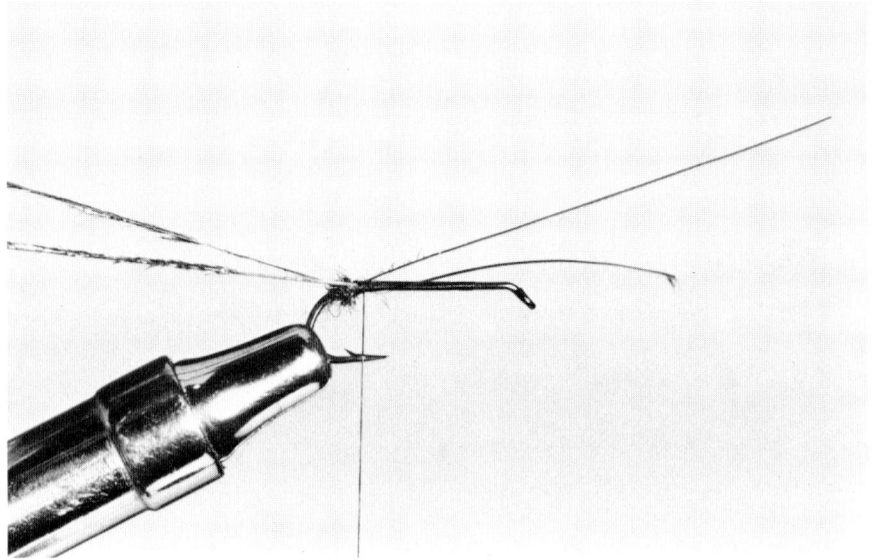

4

Bind the fibres to the shank, using ten turns of silk and working towards the right. Return to the point where the tail is attached, cut off the surplus ends of the fibres and then the surplus at the tail end so that their final length is between 1.5 and 2 cm.

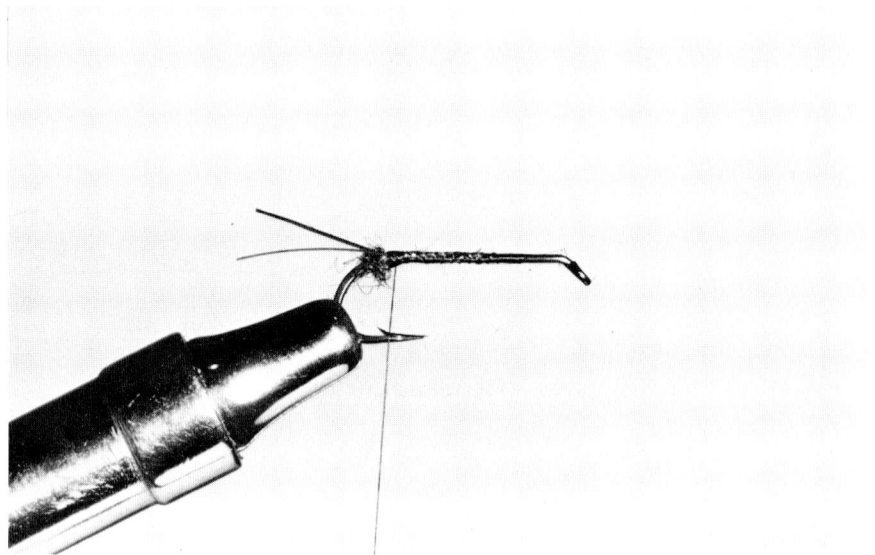

5

Wax the silk and dub it with seal fur. Wind a series of tight turns round the body of the fly, stopping two-thirds of the way along the shank. Reinforce with a half-hitch.

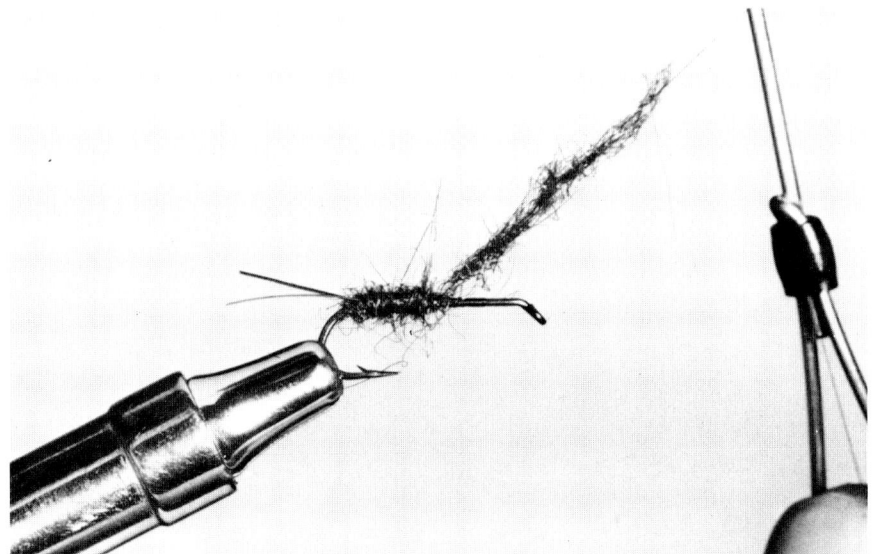

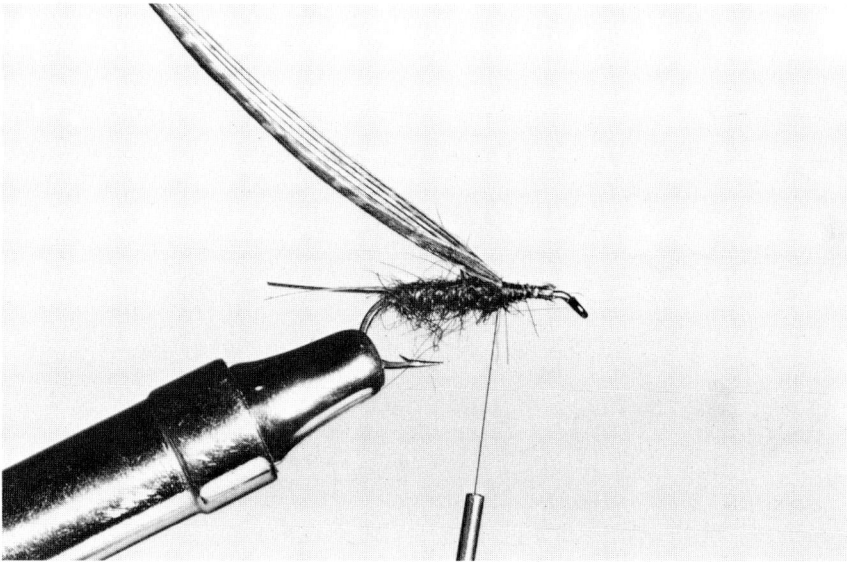

6

Take a section about 8 mm wide
from a pheasant's tail feather.
Place the outside of the feather
flat against the body of the fly.
Hold in place with several turns
of silk, finish with a half-hitch
and cut off the surplus.

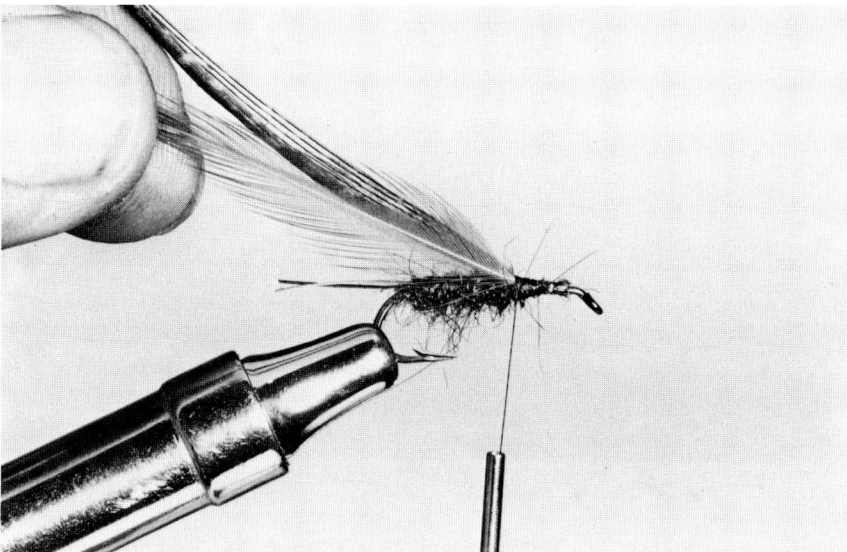

7

At the point where you attached
the pheasant's tail feather, tie in
a brown hackle. Cut off the
surplus stem and finish with a
half-hitch.

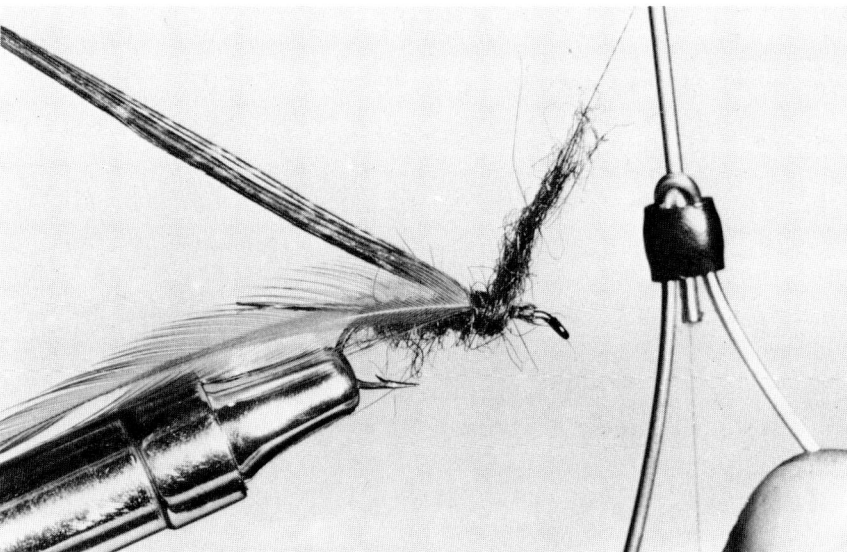

8

Wax a 2 cm length of silk and
dub it with seal hair. Construct a
thorax by making tight turns of
fur and finish with a half-hitch
2 mm from the eye.

9

Working from left to right, make three or four turns round the thorax with the hackle. Tie it in firmly. Cut off the surplus hackle and finish with a half-hitch.

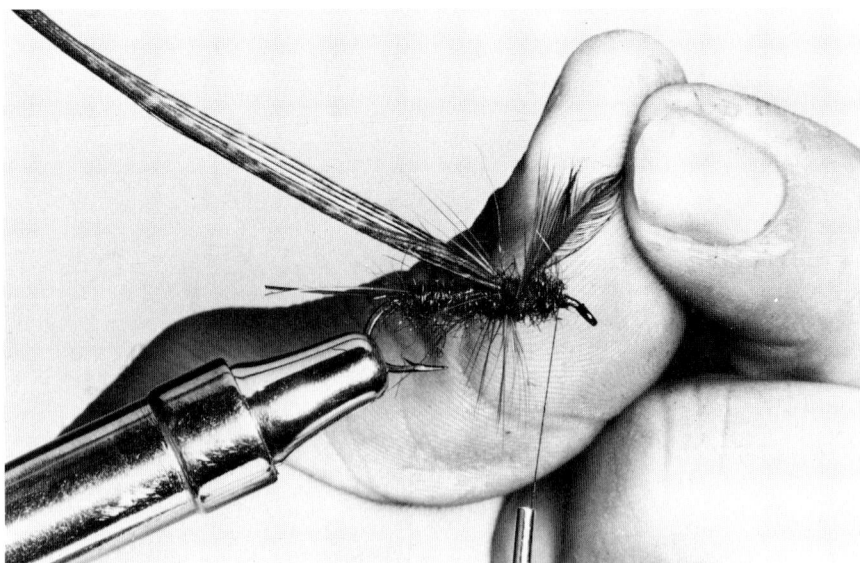

10

Taking care not to cut through the pheasant fibres, trim those of the brown hackle on top of the thorax.

11

Lower the pheasant part on top of the thorax and anchor it at the point where the hackle was tied in.

12
Cut off the surplus part of the pheasant's tail feather, make a few tight turns of silk, varnish and set aside to dry.

Jac's March Brown

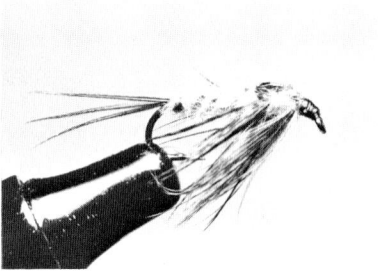

Hook: Mustad no. 3906B nos. 10 to 16
Silk: Black silk
Tail: Three fibres from a pheasant's tail feather
Body: Grey-brown fur from a hare's mask mixed with red fox fur
Ribbing: Coarse dark brown thread
Wings: Wing-case made from a section of a pheasant's tail feather
Legs: Grouse feather

1
Anchor the tying silk about 1 cm from the eye and cover the shank up to the point where the bend starts. Take three fibres from a pheasant's tail feather.

2
Tie in the fibres which will measure about 3.5 cm, and do it in such a way that they can be divided. Cut off the surplus fibres and finish with a half-hitch.

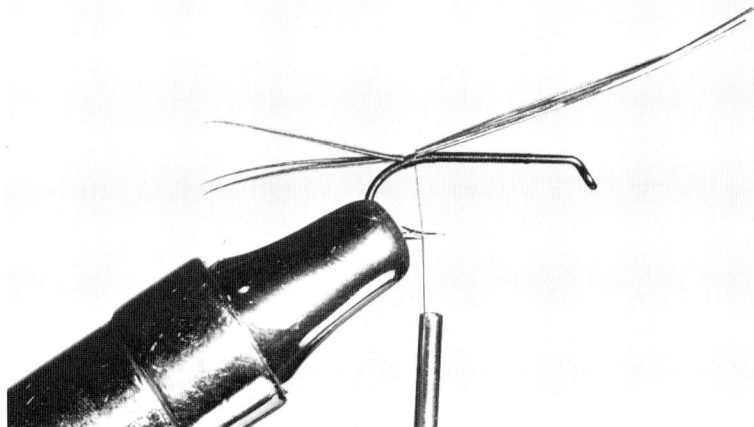

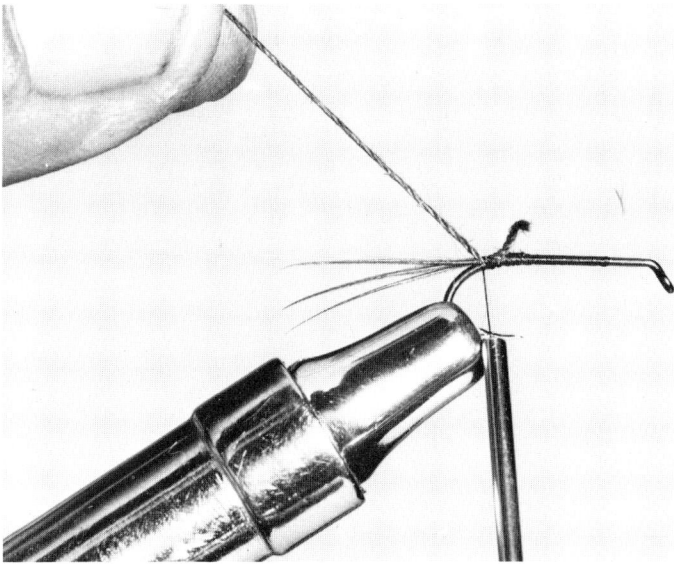

3

At this point tie in a coarse thread about 6 cm long and finish with a half-hitch.

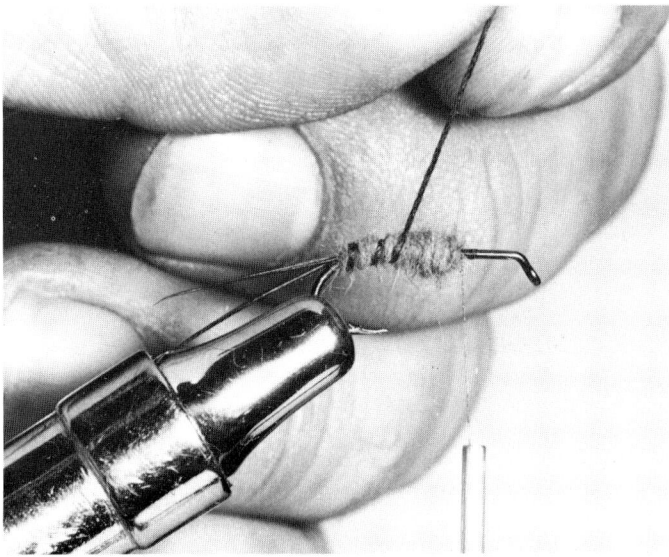

4

Construct a body using grey-brown fur from a hare's mask mixed with red fox fur and stop halfway along the shank. Divide the fly's abdomen into segments by making equidistant turns with the coarse thread. Stop at the point where the carded fur was tied in. Fasten off, cut off the surplus thread and finish with a half-hitch.

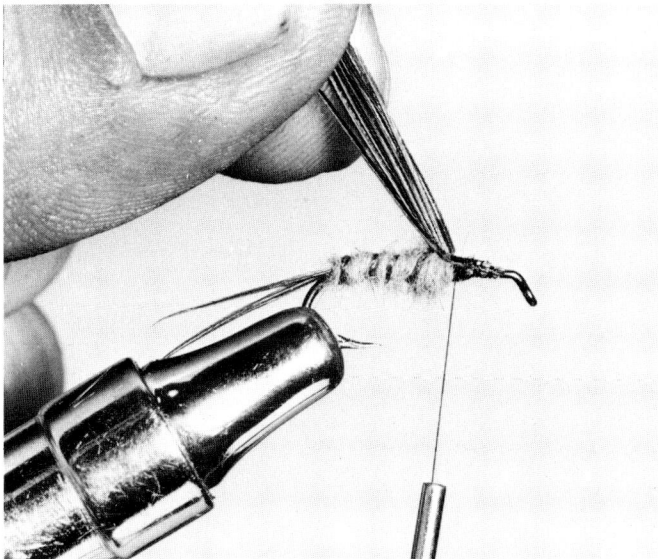

5

Pick up and tie in tightly a segment of fibres from a pheasant's tail feather. Cut off the surplus and finish with a half-hitch.

6

Take a grouse feather stripped of
its down and tie it in by the tip.
Ensure its firmness by making
several turns of silk. Cut off the
surplus and finish with a half-
hitch.

7

Wax the tying silk over a length
of 2 cm and dub it with a fur
prepared as in step 4. Starting
from this base, build up a thorax
using tight turns. Stop 2 mm
from the eye and strengthen
with a half-hitch.

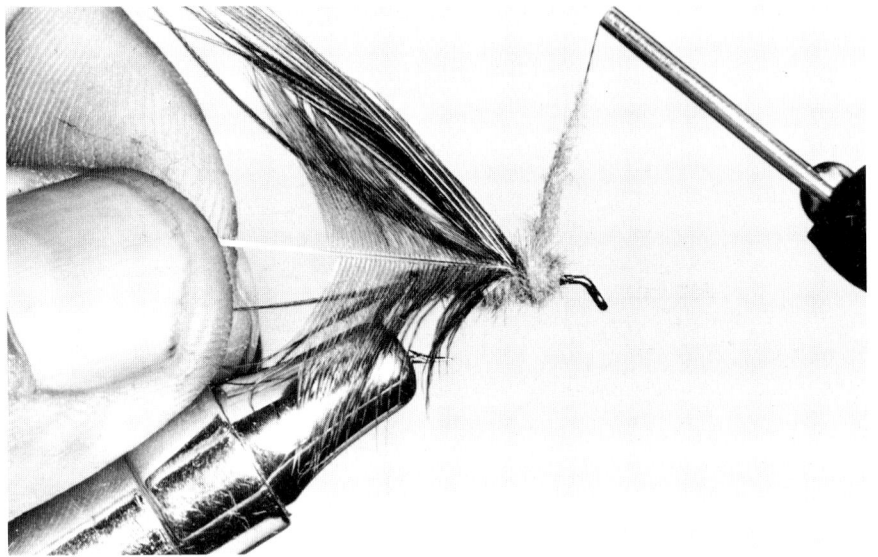

8

Using hackle pliers, grip the
quill of the grouse feather and
take it round the thorax and the
hackle itself several times at
regular intervals. Fasten off, cut
off the surplus and finish with a
half-hitch.

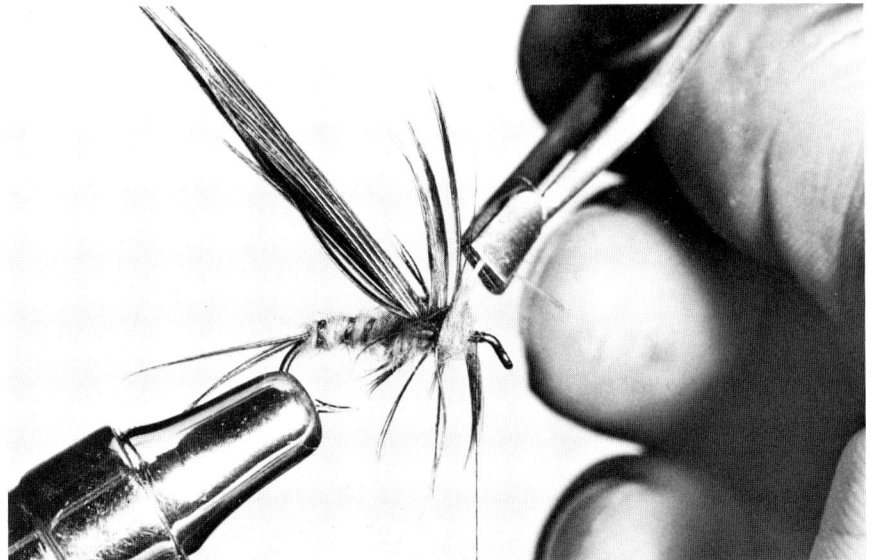

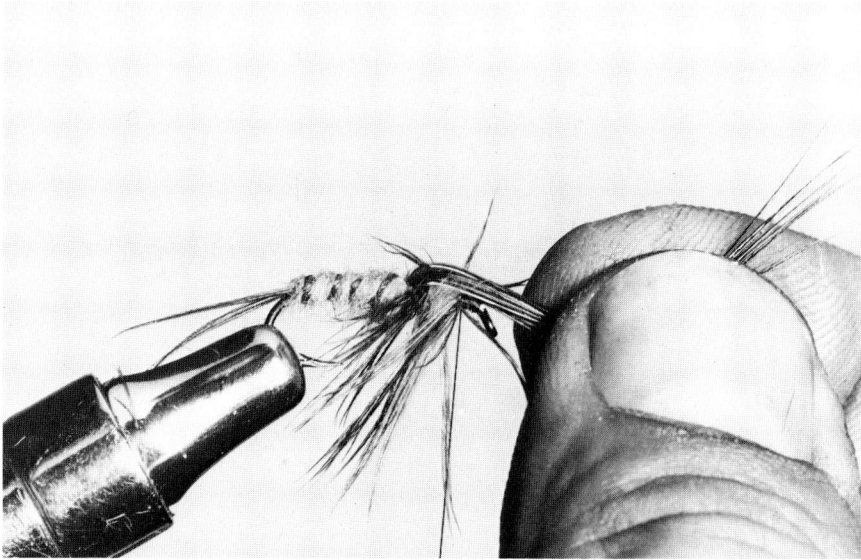

9
Form a wing-case by pulling the pheasant fibres down on to the top of the thorax. Hold the wing-case in position by making several turns of tying silk in a row.

10
Cut off the surplus fibres, reinforce with three turns of silk, proceed to the final knot, cut the silk, varnish and set aside to dry.

Chapter Seven
DRY FLIES

DRY FLIES

Dry flies are flies which are dressed to imitate adult insects at various stages. The mayfly is the insect most often imitated; it is found in the imperfect young adult state (subimago or dun), the adult state (imago), the 'spinner' or mating adult, and finally the 'spent spinner' or dead adult drifting on the surface of the water.

These flies in their classic form are dubbed with stiff hackles to improve their flotation.

In this chapter we shall deal with four dry flies, namely the Bivisible, the Blue Dun (Spider), the Hendrickson (which represents the female *Emphemerella Subvaria*) and finally the White Wulff, which has wings made from calf tail hairs.

Brown Bivisible

Hook:	Mustad no. 94840 or 94833 nos. 8 to 14
Silk:	Black silk or nylon
Tail:	Brown hackle fibres
Hackles:	Two brown hackles and one white
NOTE:	The other popular models of the Bivisible type can be tied by varying the colour of the hackles, using black, grizzly, yellow, etc.

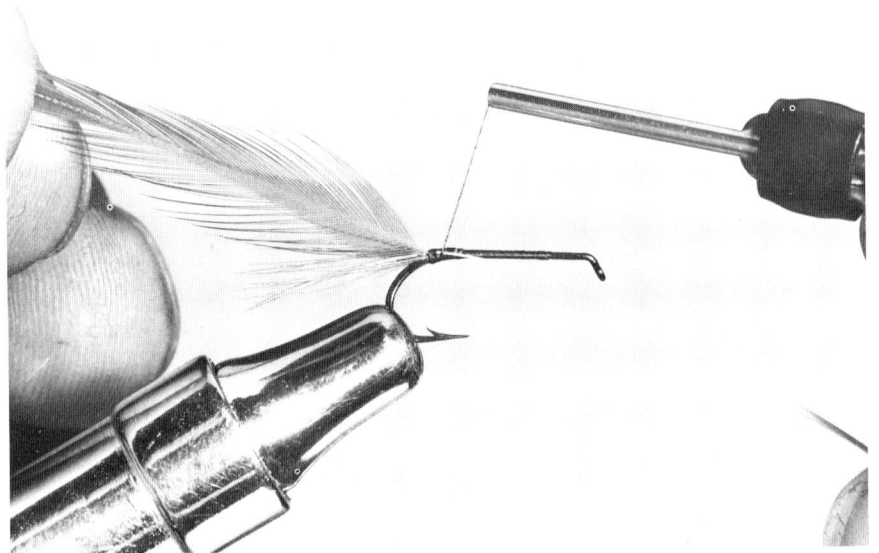

1
Anchor the tying silk, cover the shank and tie the brown hackle fibre tail in position. Strip the stem of a brown saddle hackle of its down. Attach it to the base of the fibres using several turns of tying silk and cut off the surplus stem. Reinforce with a half-hitch. Take the silk back halfway along the shank.

2
Place the tip of the hackle in the jaws of the hackle pliers, and wind down the shank with successive turns. Stop halfway along the shank and tie in with a few turns of tying silk. Reinforce with a half-hitch when you have cut off the surplus hackle.

3

When you have tied in another hackle at the same point as the first one, take the silk back to a point 6 mm from the eye.

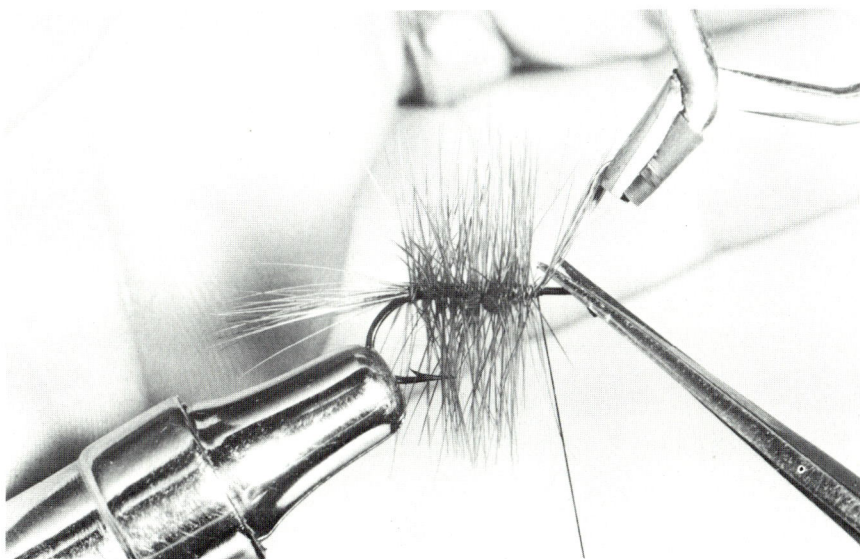

4

Proceed as shown in step 2, stopping the hackle at the point where the silk stops, namely 6 mm from the eye.

5

Using the same technique as in steps 2 and 4, proceed to tie in one white saddle hackle.

6

Grasp the tip of the hackle in the hackle pliers and turn it five times round the shank.

7

Bind the tip of the white hackle in under the silk. Cut off the surplus, ensure stability by making several turns of silk, then tie the final knot. Cut off the silk, varnish and set aside to dry.

Blue Dun (Spider)

Hook: Mustad no. 9523 or 94833 nos. 10 to 22

Silk: Black silk

Tail: Blue-dun hackle fibres

Body: Stem of grey hackle

Hackles: Blue-dun (long)

NOTE: The Spider is usually tied on a Mustad no. 9523 with the eye turned upwards.

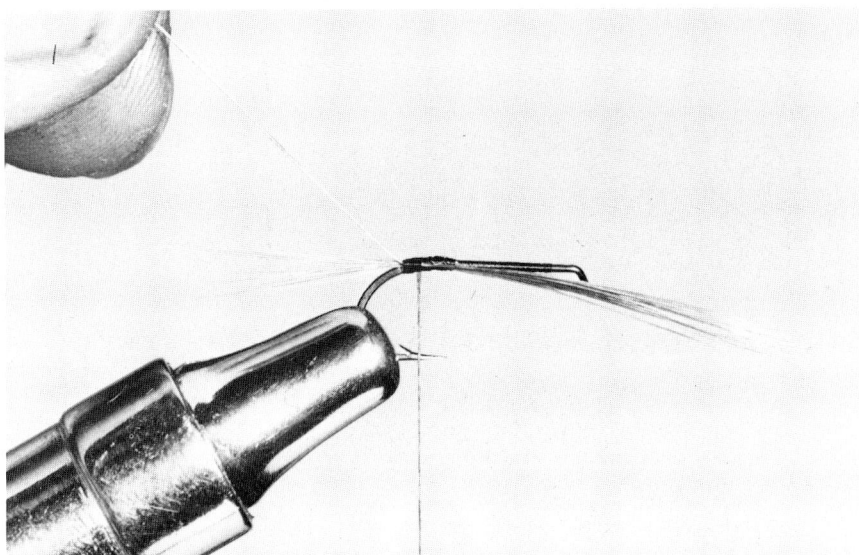

1
Anchor the tying silk in the prescribed fashion; the blue-dun hackle fibres form the tail. Strip the stem of a grey saddle hackle and tie it in by its finest tip to the point where the tail was tied in.

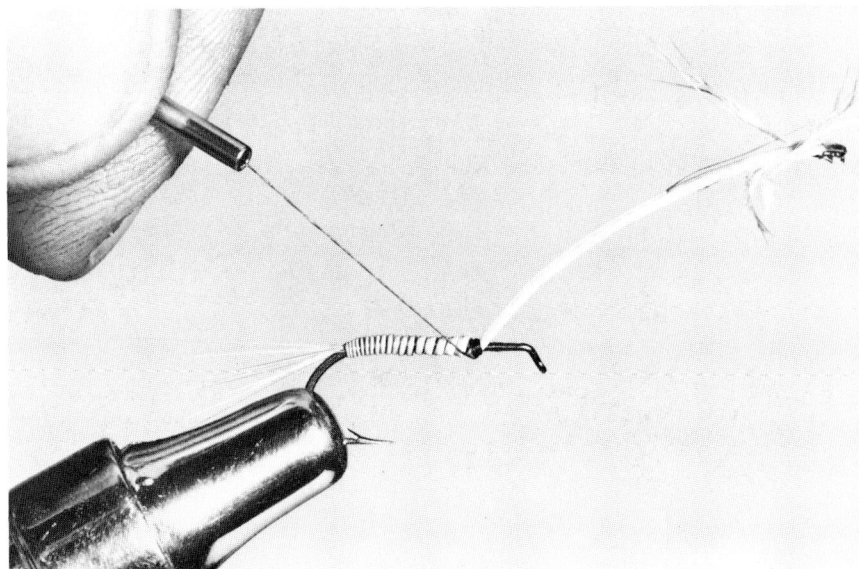

2
Wind the silk forwards and stop halfway along the body. Now bind the stem to the shank with a series of tight turns. At the point where the tying silk stops, bind the stem in with two turns of silk, then take the silk on to a point 4 mm from the eye. Follow with the stem and attach it at this point. Cut off the surplus and finish with a half-hitch.

3

At this point of attachment tie in by their stems two blue-dun saddle hackles. Fix them by binding their stems to the shank. Stop near the eye, cut off the surplus and make a half-hitch.

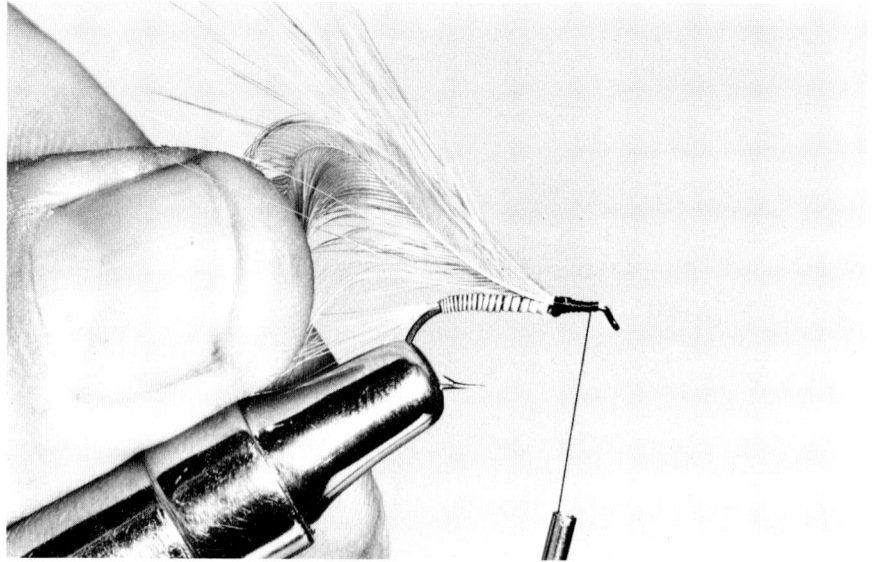

4

Using the hackle pliers, make five turns with each of the hackles and tie them in at the point of attachment in the usual fashion. Make a final knot, cut off the tying silk, varnish and set aside to dry.

5

Hendrickson

Hook:	Mustad no. 94840 or 94833 nos. 12 to 14
Silk:	Black silk
Tail:	Fibres from a crested duck flank feather or blue-dun hackle fibres
Body:	Fur from the back of the red fox or the musk rat
Hackles:	Blue-dun
Wings:	Fibres from a crested duck flank feather

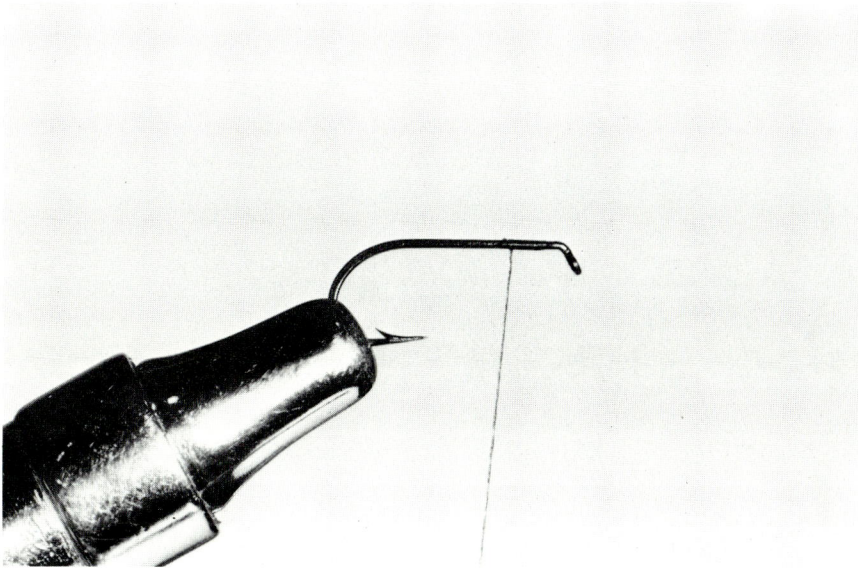

1
Anchor the tying silk to form a base 6 mm from the eye.

2
Following the procedure for mounting wings (Method 3, pages 30–32), tie in the crested duck flank feather fibres at the base point.

3

If you have followed the
prescribed method, the wings,
once in place, will look as they
do in the picture. In order to
hold them in position, apply a
drop of cement at the base.

4

Wind the tying silk back to the
start of the bend and tie in firmly
about ten blue-dun hackle fibres.
Cut off the surplus fibres and
finish with a half-hitch.

5

Return to the start of the bend,
wax the tying silk and dub it
with your choice of carded wool
selected from the suggestions
given in the pattern. Cover the
shank with this material, thus
forming a body. Stop at the end
of the wings and reinforce with a
half-hitch.

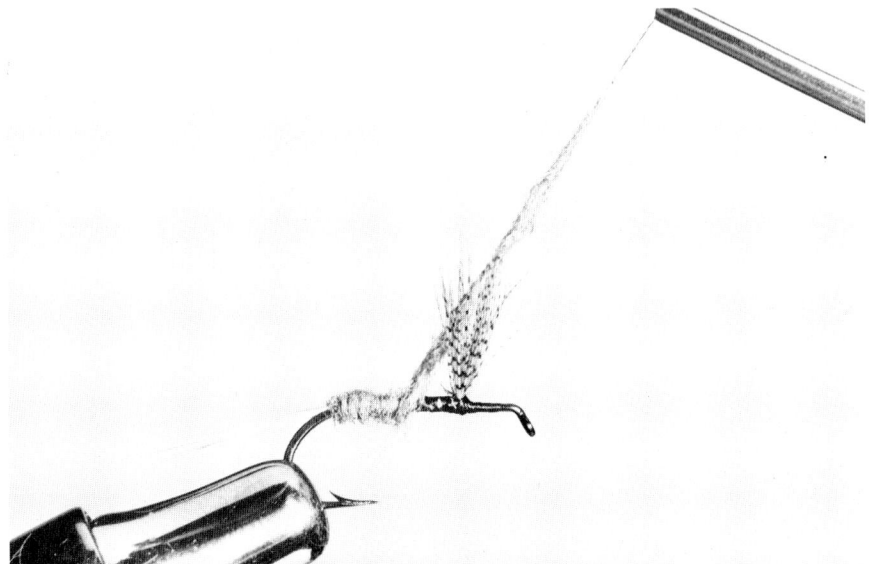

6

Select two blue–dun hackles, strip the down from their stems and anchor them firmly to the base behind the wings. Pass the silk forwards towards the eye, thus binding a part of the stems in under the tight turns. Cut off the remaining part of the stems and finish with a half–hitch.

7

Place the tip of the hackle in the jaws of your hackle pliers. With this hackle make three turns behind the wings and two turns in front of them.

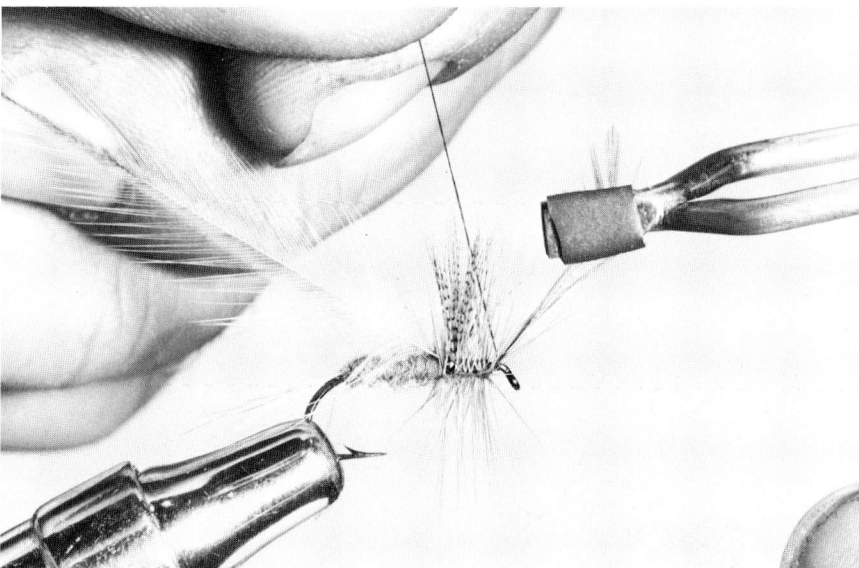

8

Tie in the hackle firmly by its remaining tip, making three turns of silk with the left hand. Cut off the surplus and finish with a half–hitch.

9

Repeat steps 7 and 8 with the second hackle.

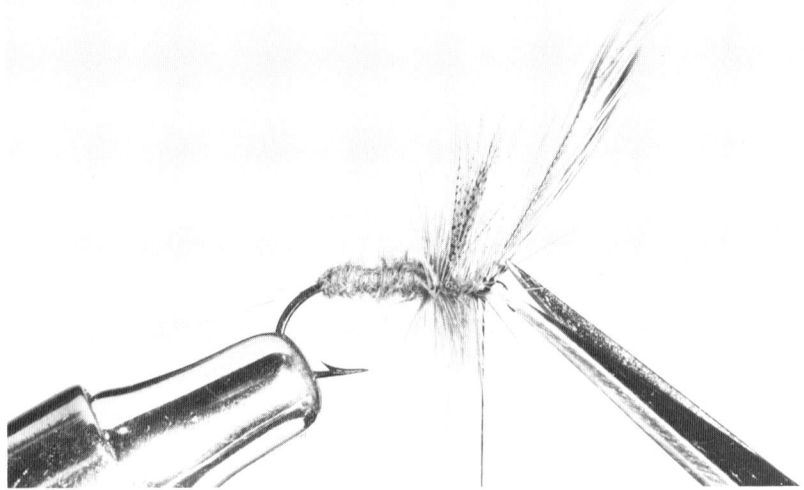

10

Having ensured that the two hackles are securely tied in, make the final knot, cut off the silk, varnish and set aside to dry.

N.B. A tightly bunched body diminishing towards the tail is to be preferred and is the mark of a high-quality fly. However, I do not believe that the trout is so choosy as to refuse to take when faced with an odd hair fibre still showing.

White Wulff

Hook: Mustad no. 94840 or 3906 nos. 6 to 16

Silk: White silk or nylon

Tail: Natural white hair (roebuck or calf tail)

Body: White mink fur

Hackles: Cream or badger

Wings: Natural white hair (roebuck or calf tail)

1
Anchor and prepare a base for the wings, using several turns of tying silk. Take a pinch of white hair from a calf's tail and tie it in at the base (see Method 5, pages 36–37).

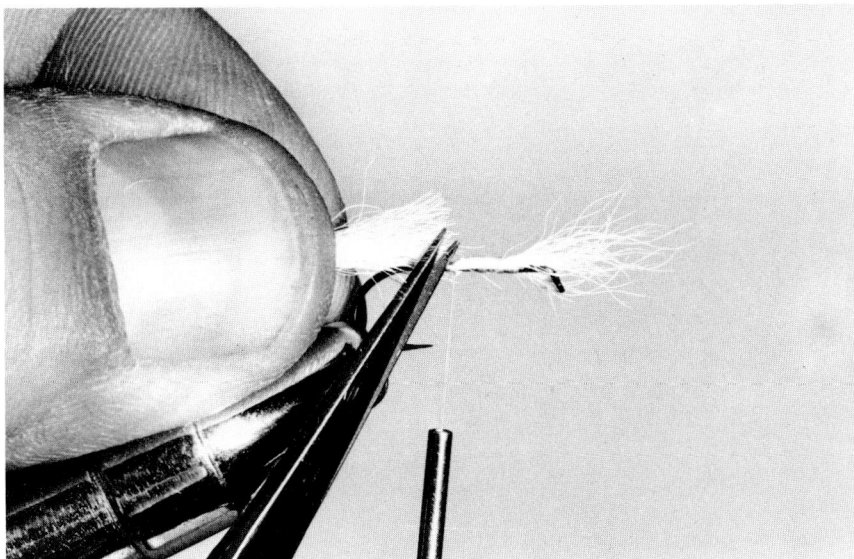

2
Bind in part of the hair up to halfway along the shank, using a series of tight turns of tying silk. Cut off the surplus.

3
Wind the tying silk back to the base and form wings, following the procedure prescribed in Method 5.

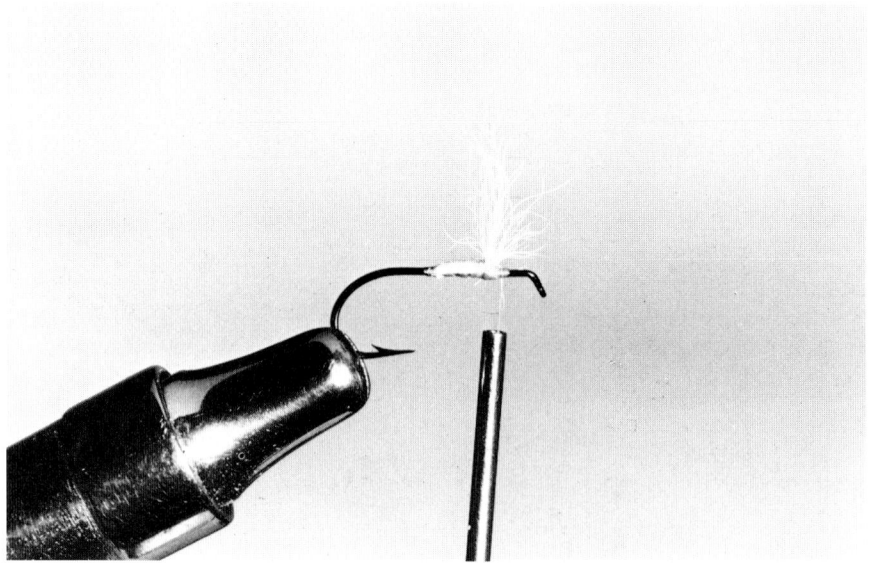

4
Take a pinch of hair from the same calf's tail and tie it in at the start of the bend. This hair, which forms the tail of the fly, should be the same length as the shank of the hook.

5
Wind the silk, binding the butts of the hairs to the shank. Stop when you reach the base of the wings, cut off the surplus hair and return towards the rear.

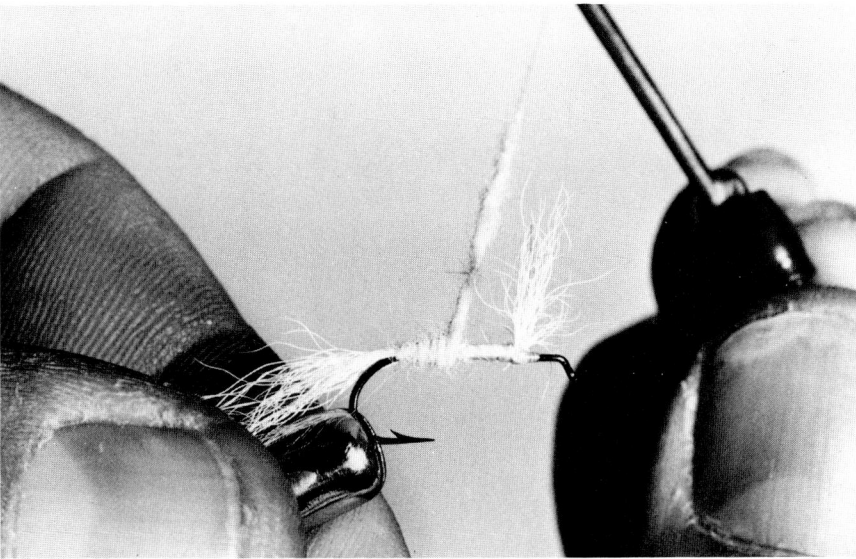

6
Wax 6 cm of tying silk and dub with mink fur. Using this material, construct a body by winding in tight turns.

7
Stop near the base of the wings, leaving a gap of about 1 mm. Hold in position with a half-hitch.

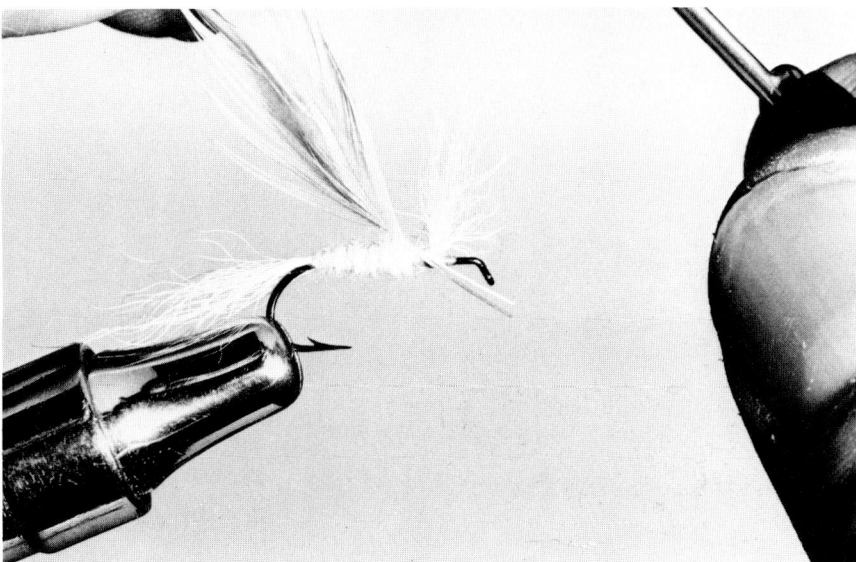

8
Select two cream or badger-coloured saddle hackles, strip them of their down and tie them in firmly by their stems behind the wings. Then pass the silk in front of the wings, thus binding in the stems.

9

Cut off the surplus stems. Grip the first hackle by the tip in the jaws of the hackle pliers. Wind three turns behind the wings and two in front, maintaining a constant pressure during this part of the work. Tie in firmly and cut off the surplus from the hackle tips.

10

Repeat this process with the second hackle and finish with a half-hitch. Proceed to the final knot, bearing in mind that the head of a dry fly must always be inconspicuous. Varnish and set aside to dry.

Chapter Eight

SPECIALS

SPECIALS

In this last chapter we look at the dressing of three flies, each of which requires stages and procedures peculiar only to itself. These are the Hornburg, the Joliette Hopper and the Muddler. These three flies are dressed in such a way that the fly-fisherman can use them equally well as dry flies, wet flies or streamers.

The Hornburg

First dressed by Frank Hornburg in Michigan in 1950 to imitate a caddis-fly, the Hornburg has widened its scope, for it has now achieved popularity with fly-fishermen in New England and Quebec.

The Joliette Hopper

The Hopper, mentioned by Walton in *The Compleat Angler* in 1653, was one of the twelve flies which every fisherman was supposed to carry in his box. Nowadays there are many patterns, the one dealt with here being a simplified version of the fly dressed by Bernard Boulard de Joliette in Quebec.

The Muddler

Don Gapen of Anoka in Minnesota, designed this fly to imitate the speckled minnow of the Nipigon River in Ontario. But for the past thirty years fly-fishermen throughout the world have been using the Muddler to imitate nymphs and land insects.

The Hornburg

Hook:	Mustad no. 9672 nos. 6 to 12 length 3x
Silk:	Black silk or nylon
Body:	Medium flat silver tinsel
Hackles:	Grizzly and wound as a brown collar
Wings:	Yellow hackle fibres with mallard flank feathers
Shoulder:	Jungle cock feather
Head:	Black

1
Anchor the tying silk in its usual position behind the eye. Proceed to tie in the tinsel in the usual way.

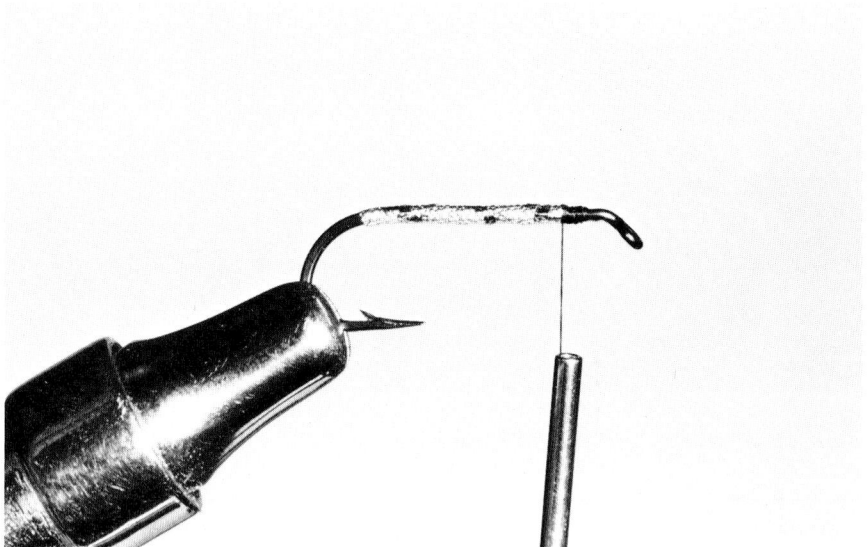

2
Take a small pinch of yellow hair from a calf's tail or a pinch of fibres from a yellow hackle.

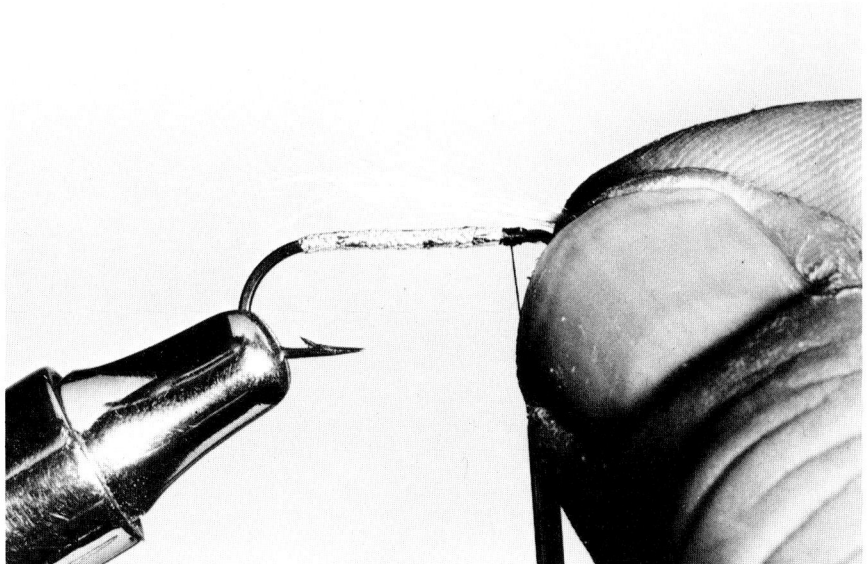

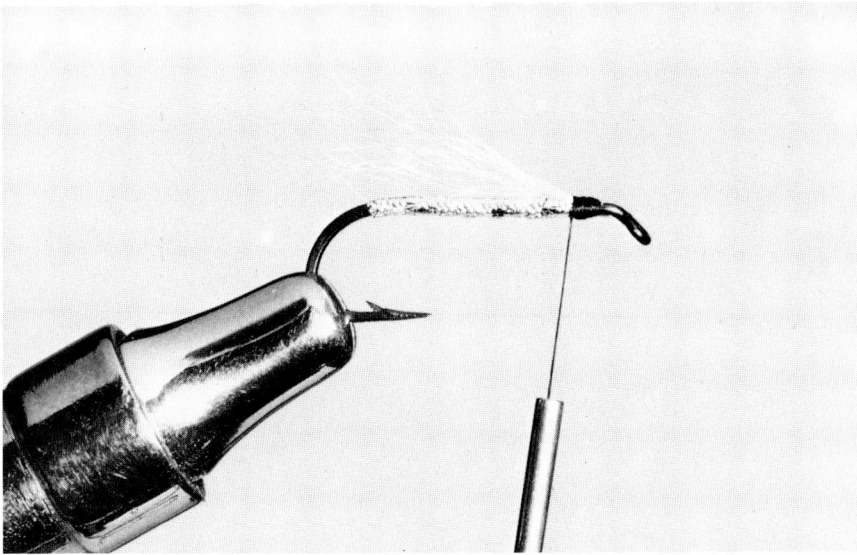

3
Tie in the selected material at the main point of attachment and reinforce with a half-hitch.

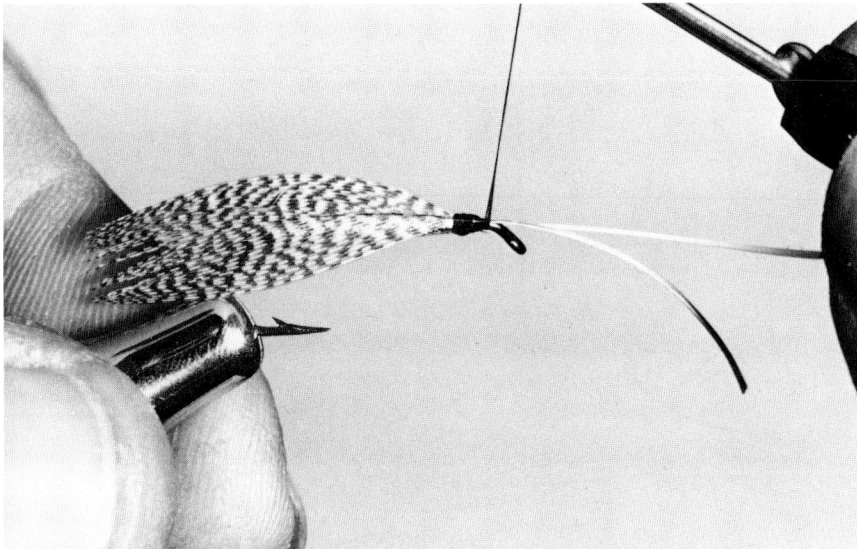

4
Select two mallard flank feathers and strip them of their down. Anchor the feathers firmly, one on either side of the hook. Cut off the surplus stems and finish with a half-hitch.

5
Now place a Jungle cock feather on either side of the wings. Tie in, cut off any surplus and finish with a half-hitch.

6
Now tie in a grizzly saddle
hackle and a brown hackle at the
point of attachment.

7
Using hackle pliers, form a collar
with these feathers. Wind five
turns, anchor, cut off the surplus
and finish with a final knot.

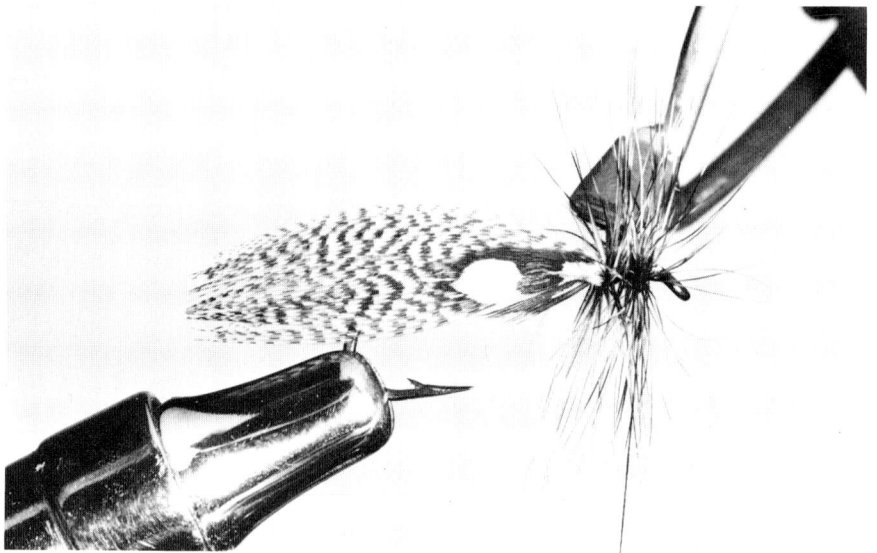

8
Apply a thin layer of transparent
varnish to the tops of the wings
and join them together. Now
varnish the whip-finish of the
head and set the fly aside to dry.

The Joliette Hopper

Hook: Mustad no. 9672 nos. 4 to 16 length 3x

Silk: Black silk or nylon

Tail: Red hackle fibres

Body: Chenille or yellow wool

Ribbing: Brown hackle

Hackles: One brown and one grizzly

Wings: Sections of speckled turkey feather

Head: Black

1
Anchor the silk on the shank 5 mm from the eye. Now wind the silk to the point where the bend of the hook begins. At this point, add a pinch of red hackle fibres.

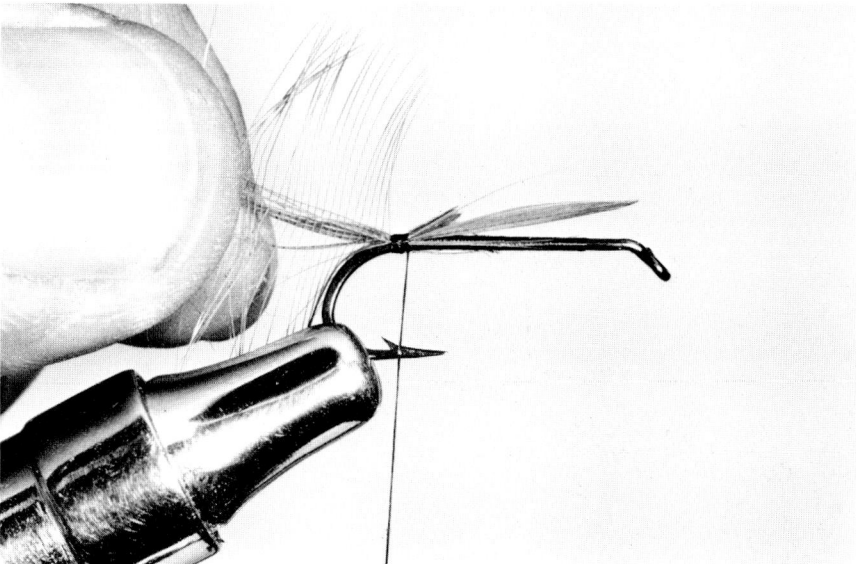

2
At this same point, tie in a brown saddle hackle by its tip.

3

At this point you should also tie
in a piece of yellow wool.

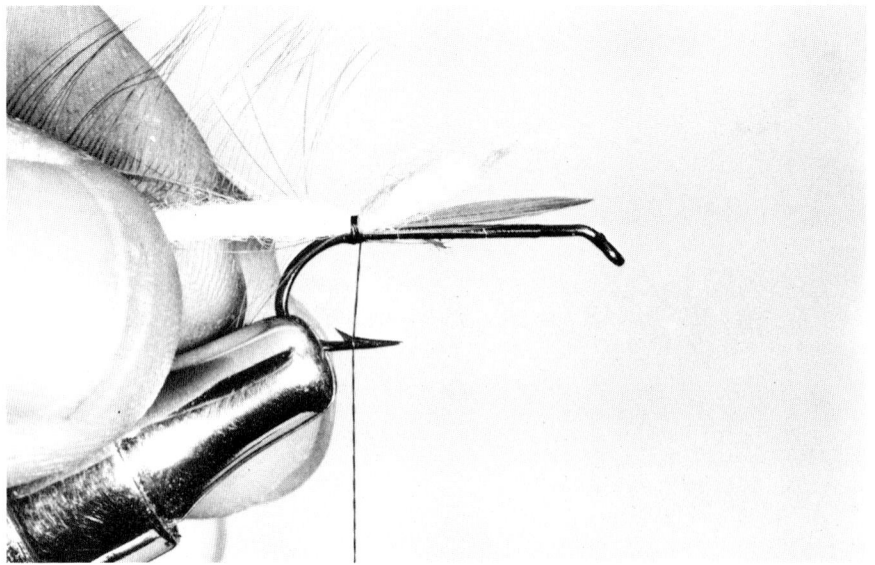

4

Wind the tying silk fowards
again till it is near the main point
of attachment. Now construct
the body of the Joliette Hopper
by winding the wool in tight
turns.

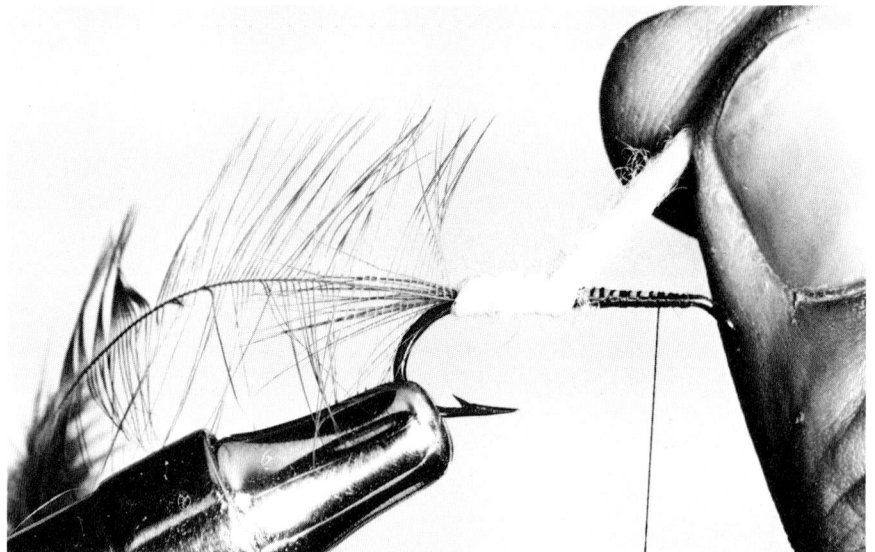

5

Anchor the wool firmly, cut off
any surplus and reinforce with a
half-hitch.

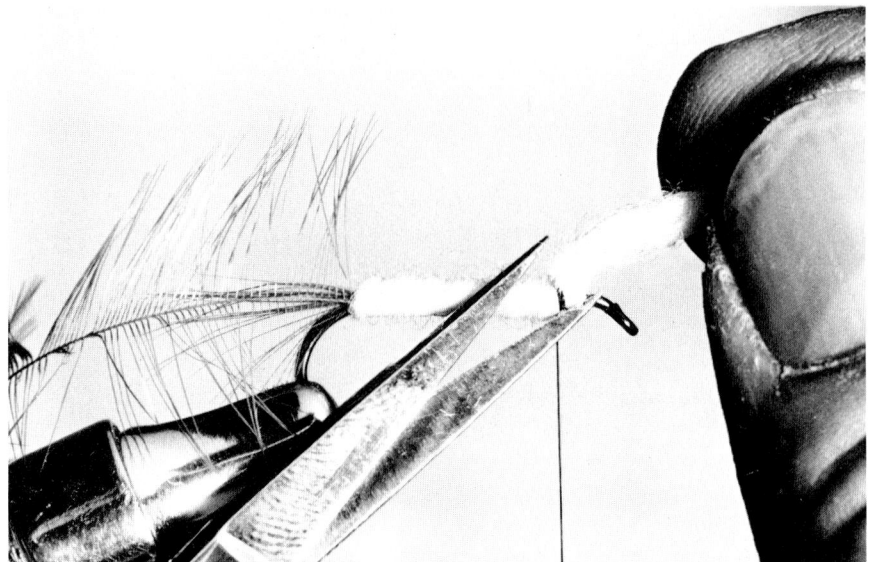

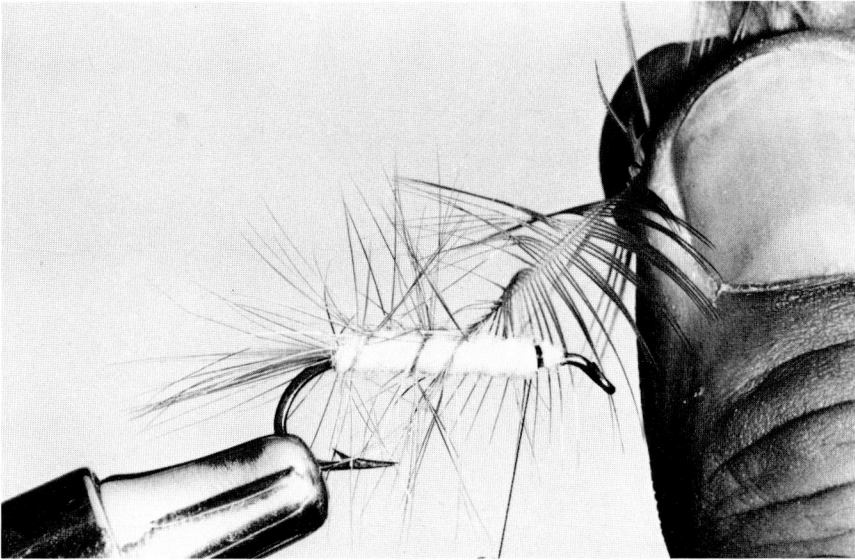

6
Wind the hackle round the body in equidistant turns, maintaining an even tension during this operation.

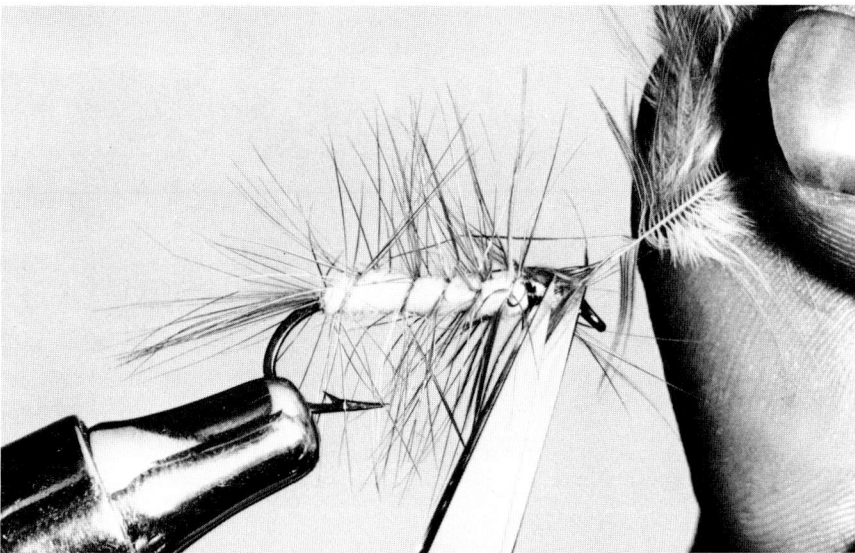

7
Stop at the point where the wool was tied in, anchor with a few turns of the silk, cut off the protruding stem and hold in position with a half-hitch.

8
Now take two matching sections from a speckled turkey feather, one from the right side and one from the left. Fix them one on either side of the body, with the tips extending 1 cm beyond the bend of the hook.

9
At this point, tie in a brown
hackle and a grizzly by their
stems. Wind the two hackles and
fasten them off in the
conventional way.

10
Cut off the surplus hackles,
make a final knot, cut the silk,
varnish the head and set the fly
aside to dry.

The Muddler

Hook:	Mustad no. 79580 or 9672 nos. 2 to 12 length 4x
Silk:	Black nylon
Tail:	Sections of speckled turkey feather
Body:	Flat gold tinsel
Wings:	Sections of speckled turkey feather with hair from the tail of a grey squirrel
Shoulder:	Hair from the back of a roebuck, flared to two-thirds of the length of the shank
Head:	Roebuck hair or trimmed caribou hair
Option:	Flat silver tinsel instead of gold

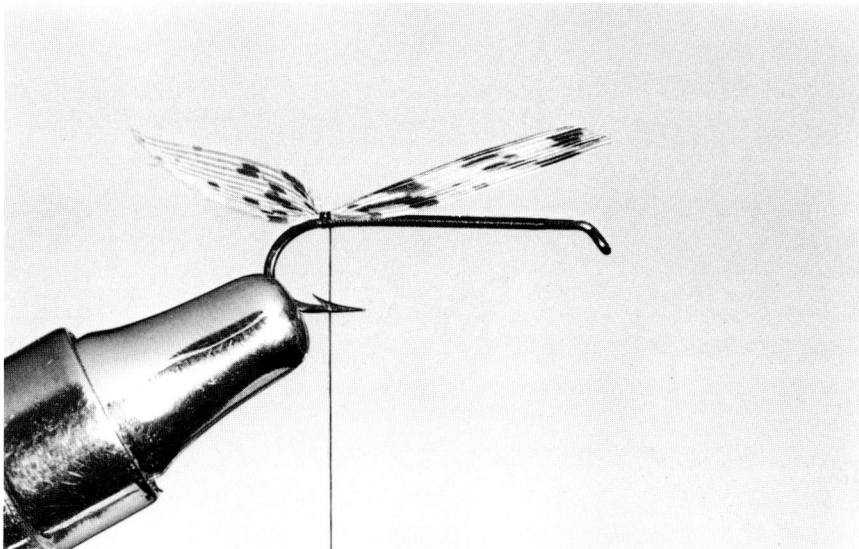

1
Anchor the tying silk about 7 mm from the eye and wind it up to the beginning of the bend. Take a section of speckled turkey feather and tie it in firmly as a tail.

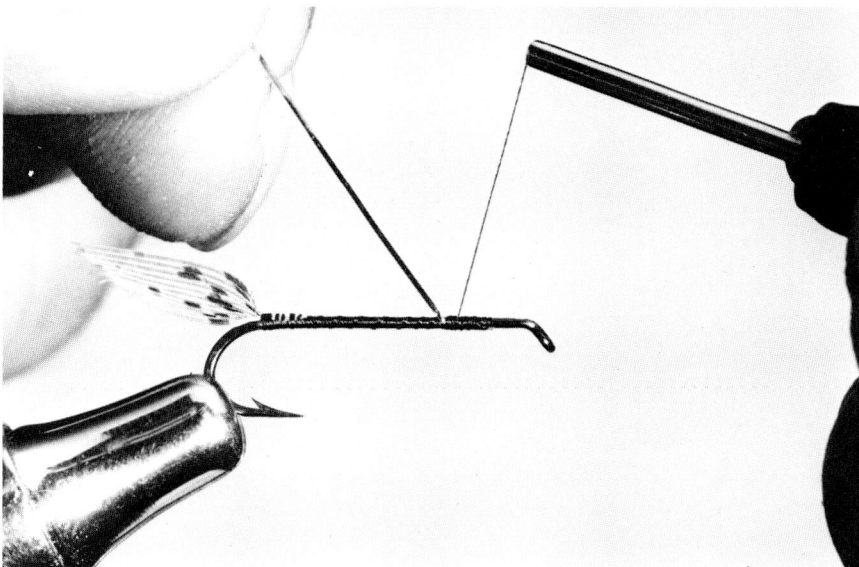

2
Returning to the starting point, tie in a piece of tinsel and reinforce it with six tight turns, winding the silk anti-clockwise.

3

Proceed to cover the shank with
the tinsel in the prescribed
manner. Return to the anchor
point and fasten securely. Cut
off the surplus thread and
reinforce with a half-hitch.

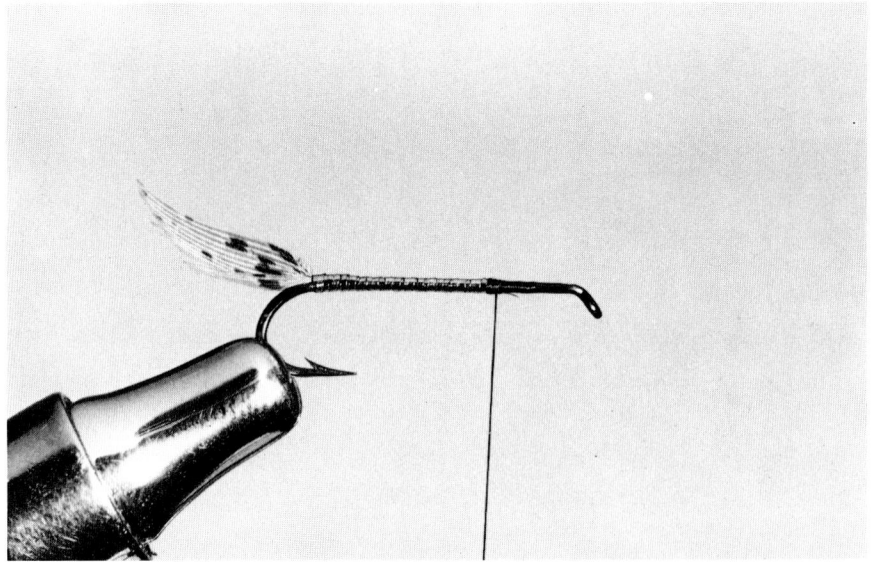

4

Take a pinch of hair from the tail
of a grey squirrel between the
thumb and index finger of the
left hand and place it on the
shank, at the point of
attachment. Tie in the hair, cut
off the surplus and hold in
position with a half-hitch.

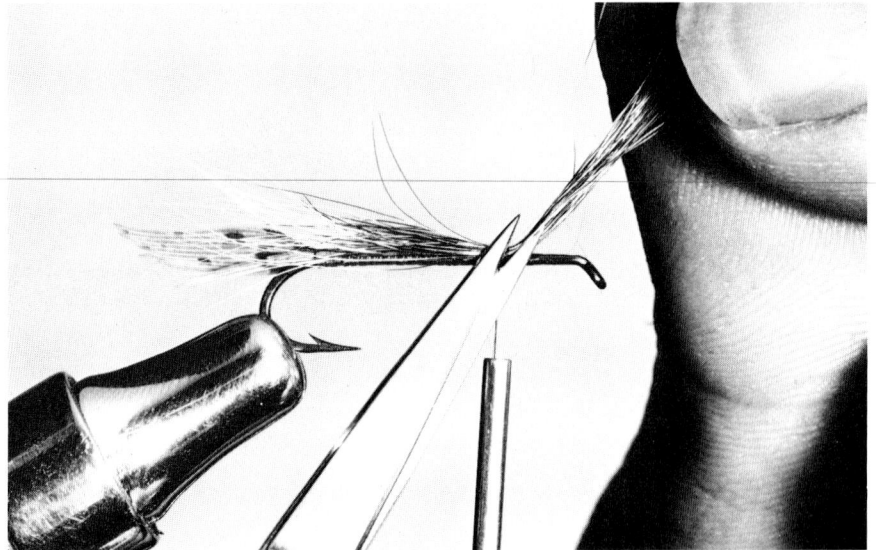

5

Cut a section from a speckled
turkey feather and fold this
section back on to itself
lengthways. Cover the squirrel
hair by tying this wing at the
point of attachment. Cut off the
surplus and add a half-hitch.

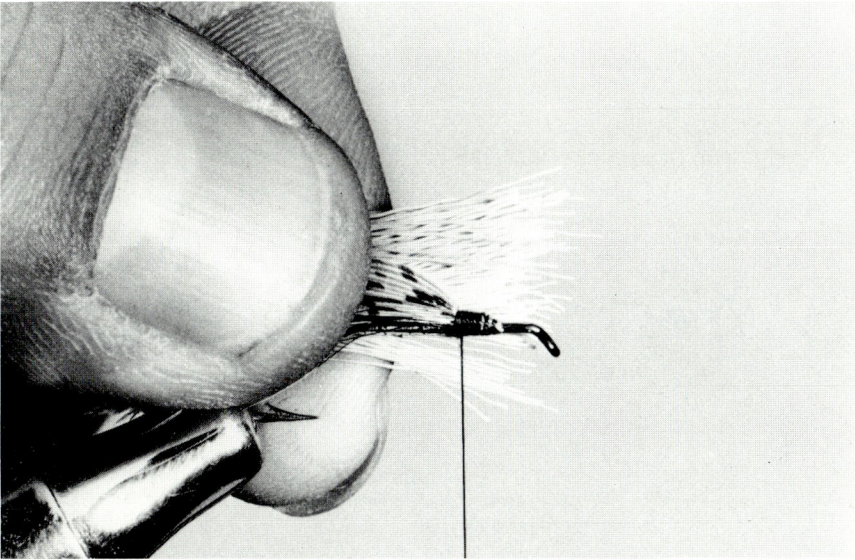

6

At this stage, take a pinch of roebuck hair. Hold the hair between the thumb and index finger of your left hand behind the eye.

7

Wind two slack turns of silk. Check that you have included all the hair, then apply a slight tension to the silk.

8

Relax your grip on the hair and increase pressure on the silk by pulling it downwards. The hair will revolve round the shank, finally settling in a fan shape.

113

9

Wind the silk out from the hair and make a few tight turns round the shank, pushing the fan of hair backwards with the fingers of the left hand. Now add a second pinch of hair, either roebuck or caribou.

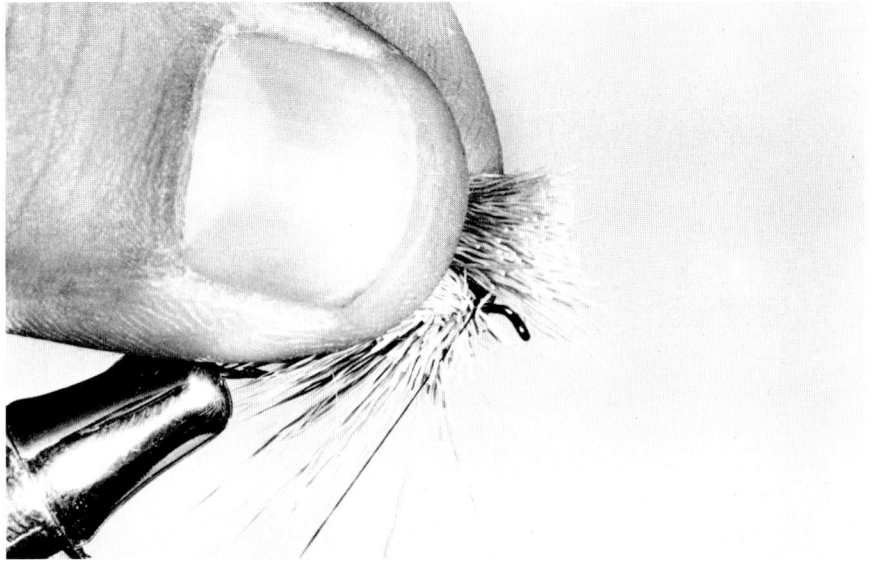

10

Using the same technique as in step 8, make a fan with this last pinch of hair.

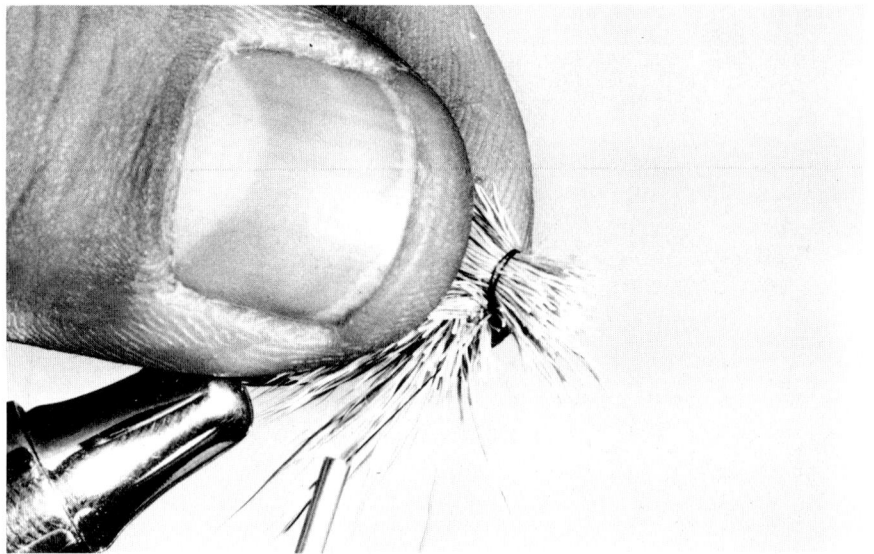

11

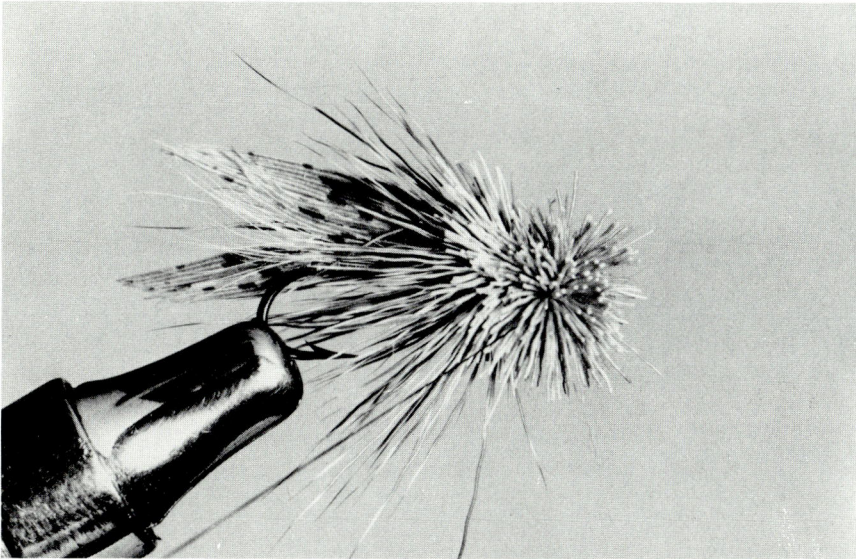

12
Wind two or three turns of silk round this second fan taking care to work between the ends of the hairs to reach the shank.

13
Pull the silk out in front of this head, make a whip-finish and cut off the surplus silk.

14
Now trim the hairy head of the Muddler as you like. Be careful not to cut the tips of the hairs surrounding the body of the fly.

115

15
When the trimming is finished, varnish the final knot. To ensure the long life of your fly, use the point of a needle to apply several drops of varnish to the roots of the head hairs.

PATTERNS

Those patterns described in detail earlier in the book are signalled by a photograph and a page reference.

BUCKTAILS

Black Nose Dace

See page 46.

Hook:	Mustad no. 3665A, 9575, 38941 or 79580 nos. 4 to 12
Silk:	Black silk or nylon
Tail:	Red wool (short)
Body:	Flat silver tinsel
Ribbing:	Optional (Oval silver tinsel)
Wings:	White roebuck or calf hair with black roebuck or bear hair with brown roebuck hair
Head:	Black
Option:	White eyes, black centre, throat of red hackle

Mickey Finn

Hook:	Mustad no. 79580 nos. 2 to 10 length 4x
Silk:	Black silk or nylon
Body:	Flat medium weight silver tinsel
Ribbing:	Oval medium weight silver tinsel
Wings:	Roebuck tail hair, yellow, with red, then yellow
Head:	Black
Option:	Eyes painted yellow, black centre

Silver Shiner

Hook:	Mustad no. 79580 nos. 6 to 10 length 4x
Silk:	Black
Body:	Flat silver tinsel
Wings:	White roebuck tail hair with dark brown
Head:	Black
Throat:	Red hackles
Option:	Eyes painted white with black centres

118

Magog Smelt

Hook:	Mustad no. 79580, 3665A or 9575 nos. 1 to 10
Silk:	Black silk or nylon
Tail:	Teal or striped mallard flank feather fibres
Body:	Flat silver tinsel
Wings:	Natural white hair with dyed yellow hair with dyed pale mauve hair (all from the tail of roebuck or calf) with six to eight fibres from a peacock's tail feather
Shoulder:	One teal flank feather on either side
Head:	Black
Throat:	Red hackle fibres
Option:	Yellow eyes with black centre

See page 50.

Nine Three

Hook:	Mustad no. 79580 or 9575 nos. 2 to 10
Silk:	Black
Body:	Flat tinsel
Wings:	White roebuck tail hair with two green saddle hackles and two black hackles
Shoulder:	Jungle cock feathers
Option:	Eyes painted yellow with black centre if Jungle cock feathers are not available and/or ribbing made from a spiral of flat silver tinsel

Supervisor

Hook:	Mustad no. 79580, 9575 nos. 2 to 8
Silk:	Black
Tail:	Red wool
Body:	Flat silver tinsel
Ribbing:	Spiral of oval silver tinsel
Wings:	White roebuck tail hair with four blue saddle hackles and, on either side of the blue hackles, a green hackle half the length of the blue with five or six peacock tail feathers as topping
Shoulder:	Jungle cock feathers
Head:	Black
Throat:	Blue hackle
Option:	Eyes painted yellow with black centre if Jungle cock feathers are not available

STREAMERS

Grey Ghost

See page 53.

Hook:	Mustad no. 9575 nos. 2 to 12
Silk:	Black
Tag:	Flat silver tinsel
Body:	Orange floss silk
Ribbing:	Spiral of flat silver tinsel
Wings:	Four grey saddle hackles
Shoulder:	Silver pheasant flank feathers with Jungle cock
Head:	Black
Throat:	Peacock tail feathers, white roebuck tail hair and fibres from a golden pheasant crest feather
Option:	Red collar to the head (original), yellow eyes with black centre if Jungle cock feathers are not available

Black Ghost

Hook:	Mustad no. 9575 or 3665A nos. 2 to 12 length 6x
Silk:	Black
Tail:	Yellow hackle fibres
Body:	Black floss silk
Ribbing:	Flat silver tinsel
Wings:	Four white hackles (from saddle or neck of cock)
Shoulder:	Jungle cock feathers
Head:	Black
Throat:	Yellow hackle fibres
Option:	Underwings in white roebuck tail hair and wings in white marabou sections

Green Ghost

Hook:	Mustad no. 9575 nos. 2 to 12 length 6x
Silk:	Black
Tag:	Flat silver tinsel
Body:	Orange floss silk
Ribbing:	Flat silver tinsel
Wings:	Two green saddle hackles with two black hackles
Shoulder:	Silver pheasant flank feathers with Jungle cock feathers either side
Head:	Black
Throat:	Peacock tail fibres, white roebuck tail hair with golden pheasant crest fibres
Option:	Eyes painted yellow if Jungle cock feathers are not available

Hook: Mustad no. 79580 nos. 6 to 12 length 4x

Royal Coachman

Silk: Black silk or nylon

Tail: Tippet of golden pheasant

Body: Front and rear of the body are made of peacock tail feathers, the middle is in red floss silk

Wings: Four white hackles (neck or saddle)

Head: Black

Throat: Brown hackle

Hook: Mustad no. 9672 nos. 2 to 10 length 4x

Dark Spruce Fly

Silk: Black

Tail: Three peacock sword feather fibres

Body: Red floss silk and front of peacock tail feather fibres

Ribbing: Embossed gold tinsel

Wings: Four rust-brown saddle hackles

Head: Black

Throat: Collar of rust-brown hackle

Hook: Mustad no. 9672 nos. 2 to 10 length 4x

Light Spruce Fly

Silk: Black

Tail: Three peacock sword feather fibres

Body: Red floss silk with front of peacock tail feather fibres (peacock herl)

Ribbing: Embossed gold tinsel

Wings: Four badger-coloured hackles

Head: Black

Throat: Collar of badger-coloured hackle

WET FLIES

Dark Hendrickson

See page 60.

Hook:	Mustad no. 9671 nos. 10 to 14
Silk:	Black silk or nylon
Tail:	Fibres of blue-dun hen hackle, or crested duck flank feather fibres
Body:	Grey musk rat fur
Throat:	Fibres of blue-dun hen hackle
Wings:	Crested duck flank feather fibres

Dark Cahill

Hook:	Mustad no. 9671 or 9672 nos. 8 to 14
Silk:	Brown silk
Tail:	Brown hackle fibres
Body:	Dark grey musk rat fur
Throat:	Brown hackle fibres
Wings:	Crested duck flank feather fibres

Light Cahill

Hook:	Mustad no. 9671 or 9672 nos. 8 to 14
Silk:	Yellow silk
Tail:	Crested duck flank feather fibres
Body:	Cream red fox belly fur or faded racoon fur as substitute
Throat:	Pale rust hen hackle fibres
Wings:	Crested duck flank feather fibres or dyed mallard

Hook: Mustad no. 9671 nos. 10 to 14

Silk: 'Tan' silk

Tail: Blue-dun hackle fibres or crested duck flank feather fibres

Body: Cream coloured fox or racoon fur, faded and mixed with a pinch of hair from a hare if the pink urine-stained fur from the belly of the red fox is not available

Throat: Blue-dun hen hackle fibres

Wings: Crested duck or dyed mallard flank feather fibres

Hook: Mustad no. 7957BX nos. 12 to 14

Silk: Black silk

Tail: Blue-dun hackle fibres

Body: Peacock tail feather quill, stripped

Ribbing: Very fine gold oval tinsel

Throat: Blue-dun hen hackle fibres

Wings: Crested duck flank feather fibres

Hook: Mustad no. 9671 nos. 12 to 14

Silk: Black silk or nylon

Tag: Optional. Flat gold tinsel

Tail: None

Body: Very thick bronze peacock herl

Throat: Brown hackle fibres

Wings: Section of white duck or goose feathers

See page 64.

Black Gnat

Hook:	Mustad no. 9671 nos. 10 to 14
Silk:	Black nylon
Tail:	Optional. Hackle fibres dyed black or red
Body:	Black chenille or rabbit fur dyed black
Throat:	Hackle fibres dyed black
Wings:	Two segments of grey duck feather

Blue Dun

Hook:	Mustad no. 9671 nos. 10 to 18
Silk:	Black silk
Tail:	Medium blue-dun hackle fibres
Body:	Grey musk rat fur
Throat:	Blue-dun hackle feathers (hen)
Wings:	Sections from grey goose or duck feathers

Blue Winged Olive

Hook:	Mustad no. 9671 or 9672 nos. 10 to 14
Silk:	Olive silk
Tail:	Grey hackle fibres
Body:	Hare, beaver or mink fur dyed olive
Throat:	Medium blue-dun hackle fibres
Wings:	Sections of grey feathers, goose or duck

Hook: Mustad no. 9671 or 7957BX nos. 6 to 14   **Dark Montreal**

Silk: Black silk or nylon

Tail: Sections of duck feather, dyed red

Body: Floss silk. Claret colour

Ribbing: Flat gold tinsel

Throat: Hen hackle fibres dyed claret

Wings: Sections of speckled turkey feather

Hook: Mustad no. 9671 or 7957BX nos. 12 to 14   **Ginger Quill**

Silk: Black silk

Tail: Rust hackle fibres

Body: Stripped peacock quill

Throat: Rust hackle fibres (hen)

Wings: Sections of grey feathers, duck or goose

Hook: Mustad no. 9671 or 7957BX nos. 6 to 16   **Gold Ribbed Hare's Ear**

Silk: Black silk or nylon

Tail: Brown hackle fibres

Body: Hare's mask fur (cheek and ear)

Ribbing: Flat gold tinsel, fine

Throat: Thorax; picked out with the aid of a needle or bodkin

Wings: Sections of natural grey mallard quill feathers

WET FLIES

Leadwing Coachman

Hook:	Mustad no. 9671 nos. 10 to 14
Silk:	Black silk or nylon
Tag:	Flat gold tinsel instead of tail, or
Tail:	Brown hackle
Body:	Peacock herl, bronze
Throat:	Dark brown hackle fibres
Wings:	Sections of grey feathers, goose or duck

March Brown

Hook:	Mustad no. 9671 nos. 10 to 12
Silk:	Black silk
Tail:	Brown partridge feather fibres or tufted duck or grouse
Body:	Hare's mask fur (pale brown)
Ribbing:	Flat gold tinsel or yellow silk
Throat:	Same fibres as used to make tail
Wings:	Sections of speckled turkey feathers

Parmachene Belle

Hook:	Mustad no. 9671 nos. 10 to 14
Silk:	Black silk or nylon
Tail:	Hackle fibres, mixed red and white
Body:	Yellow floss silk
Ribbing:	Flat silver tinsel
Throat:	Red and white hackle fibres
Wings:	In three sections, two sections white, and one red in the centre, make from duck or goose feathers

Hook: Mustad no. 3906 or 3906B nos. 8 to 12

Silk: Black silk

Body: White hare fur

Thorax: Castor fur dyed black

Hackle: Guinea hen neck feather

S.J.V. Caddis

See page 72.

Hook: Mustad no. 94840 nos. 14 to 18

Silk: Black silk

Tail: Black hackle fibres

Body: Stripped peacock quill

Throat: Thorax of black hackle, trimmed top and bottom

NOTE: Several other colour variations are popular: grizzly, grey, brown and olive

Midge (Black)

Hook: Mustad no. 9671 or 3906 nos. 8 to 14

Silk: Black silk or nylon

Tail: Sections of red duck feather

Body: Peacock herl, bronze

Hackle: Brown hackle

Brown Hackle

127

NYMPHS

Green Caddis Pupa

Hook:	Mustad no. 3906 or 3906B nos. 8 to 16
Silk:	Brown silk
Body:	Hare fur mixed with seal fur dyed green
Ribbing:	Spiral of coarse olive silk
Wings:	Trimmed on the side with wing or primary feathers of grey mallard
Throat:	The throat and legs are made of partridge feather fibres
Head:	Two or three green ostrich feather fibres
NOTE:	Several other colour variations are popular: grey, olive, yellow, etc.

Grey Nymph

Hook:	Mustad no. 79580 nos. 6 to 12 length 4x
Silk:	Grey silk
Tail:	Hair from a grey squirrel's tail
Body:	Pale grey hare fur
Hackle:	Grizzly hackle, wound as a collar, but sloping backwards

Midge Pupa

Hook:	Mustad 3906B nos. 10 to 28
Silk:	Black silk
Tail:	Optional. Black hackle fibres
Body:	Stripped peacock quill
Throat:	Thorax in black fur with five or six black hackle fibres as legs

Hook:	Mustad no. 79580 nos. 6 to 12 length 4x
Silk:	Black nylon
Tail:	Two stripped peacock tail quills
Body:	Seal fur, claret colour
Wings:	Wing-case made from section of dark turkey feather
Legs:	Brown hackle

Jac's Red Stone

See page 75.

Hook:	Mustad no. 79580 nos. 6 to 12 length 4x
Silk:	Black nylon
Tail:	Two peacock tail feather fibres
Body:	Rabbit fur dyed black
Wings:	Wing-case made from section of dark turkey feather
Legs:	Black hackle

Jac's Black Stone

Hook:	Mustad no. 79580 nos. 6 to 12 length 4x
Silk:	Black nylon
Tail:	Two stripped peacock tail feather quills
Body:	Brown musk rat fur
Wings:	Wing-case made from sections of dark turkey feather
Legs:	Brown hackle

Jac's Brown Stone

NYMPHS

Jac's Grey Stone

Hook:	Mustad no. 79580 nos. 6 to 12 length 4x
Silk:	Black silk
Tail:	Two stripped peacock tail feather quills
Body:	Grey musk rat fur
Wings:	Wing-case made from sections of dark turkey feather
Legs:	Brown hackle

Large Black Stone Fly

Hook:	Mustad no. 79580 nos. 1 to 8 length 4x
Silk:	Brown nylon
Tail:	Two peccary hairs
Body:	Mixed black and brown fur
Ribbing:	Brown spiral, coarse silk or monofilament
Wings:	Two trimmed wing-cases made from a brown partridge feather
Head:	Brown with a pair of antennae made from what is left over of the brown partridge feather used for the wing-case
Legs:	Grouse hackle fibres

Jac's March Brown

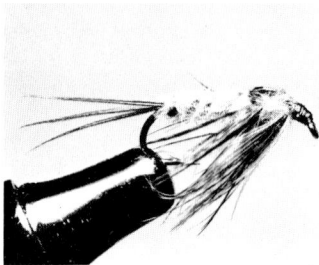

Hook:	Mustad no. 3906 nos. 10 to 16
Silk:	Black silk
Tail:	Three pheasant tail feather fibres
Body:	Grey brown fur from a hare's mask mixed with red fox fur
Ribbing:	Coarse dark brown silk
Wings:	Wing-case made from cock pheasant tail fibres
Legs:	Grouse feather

See page 80.

		Blue Quill Nymph
Hook:	Mustad no. 9671 nos. 16 to 18	
Silk:	Black silk	
Tail:	Three hairs from an elk's back	
Body:	Stripped stem of blue-dun hackle	
Wings:	Wing-case made from a crow's wing feather	
Legs:	Blue-dun hackle (hen)	

		Hare's Ear
Hook:	Mustad no. 9671 or 3906 nos. 8 to 14	
Silk:	Black silk	
Tail:	Brown hackle fibres or mallard flank feather fibres	
Body:	Fur and hair from a hare's mask	
Ribbing:	Flat gold tinsel	
Wings:	Wing-case of sections of natural mallard quill feather	
Legs:	Hair and fur picked out with the aid of a needle	

		Hendrickson
Hook:	Mustad no. 9671 or 3906B nos. 12 to 16 length 2X	
Silk:	Olive silk	
Tail:	Bunch of crested duck flank feather fibres	
Body:	Grey-brown fur (mixture of beaver, musk rat and seal hair, claret colour)	
Ribbing:	Brown silk or gold brocade	
Wings:	Wing-case of brown turkey feather or grey goose feather	
Legs:	Brown partridge feather fibres	

March Brown

Hook: Mustad no. 3906B nos. 12 to 14

Silk: Black silk

Tail: Bronze mallard flank feather fibres

Body: Grey-brown hair from a hare's mask

Wings: Dark brown mink tail hairs

Throat: Thorax made from brown hare's mask fur or dark red fox

American March Brown

Hook: Mustad no. 3906B nos. 10 to 16

Silk: Black silk

Tail: Three to five hairs from an elk's back

Body: Tobacco-coloured floss silk

Ribbing: Stripped peacock tail quill

Wings: Wing-case made from section of speckled turkey feather

Throat: Thorax made from peacock herl and legs from brown hackle

March Brown (Flick)

Hook: Mustad no. 9671 or 3906B no. 10

Silk: Brown silk

Tail: Three pheasant tail feather fibres

Body: Red fox fur mixed with amber coloured seal fur

Ribbing: Brown silk

Wings: Wing-case made from pheasant's tail feather

Legs: Brown partridge feather fibres

Hook:	Mustad no. 9671 or 9672 nos. 6 to 12 length 2x
Silk:	Black silk or nylon
Tail:	Three fibres from a peacock's sword feather
Ribbing:	Flat silver tinsel
Wings:	Wing-case, trimmed mallard flank feather
Legs:	Brown hackle

Zug Bug

DRY FLIES

Hook:	Mustad no. 94840 or 94833 nos. 8 to 14
Silk:	Black silk or nylon
Tail:	Brown hackle fibres
Hackles:	Two brown hackles and one white one
NOTE:	You may also dress other popular Bivisible patterns by changing the colour of the hackles to black, grizzly, yellow, etc.

Brown Bivisible

See page 88.

Blue Dun (Spider)

Hook:	Mustad no. 94840 or 94833 nos. 10 to 22
Silk:	Black silk
Tail:	Blue-dun hackle fibres
Body:	Stem of brown hackle
Hackles:	Blue-dun (long)
NOTE:	The Spider is usually tied on Mustad no. 9523 with the eye turned up

See page 91.

Blue Winged Olive

Hook:	Mustad no. 94840 or 94833 nos. 16 to 24
Silk:	Olive silk
Tail:	Blue-dun hackle fibres
Body:	Dyed olive hare fur mixed with sulphur yellow hare hairs
Hackles:	Medium blue-dun

Cream Variant

Hook:	Mustad no. 94838 no. 12 (short)
Silk:	Yellow silk
Tail:	Long cream hackle fibres
Body:	Stripped cream hackle stem
Hackles:	Two (cream)

Dun Variant

Hook:	Mustad no. 94838 nos. 10 to 12
Silk:	Olive silk
Tail:	Blue-dun hackle fibres
Body:	Stripped brown hackle stem
Hackles:	One dark blue-dun

		Blue Quill
Hook:	Mustad no. 94840 or 94833 nos. 12 to 20	
Silk:	Black silk	
Tail:	Blue-dun hackle fibres	
Body:	Stripped peacock quill	
Ribbing:	Optional. Very fine gold brocade	
Hackles:	Two blue-dun	
Wings:	Grey duck feathers	

		Ginger Quill
Hook:	Mustad no. 94840 or 94833 nos. 12 to 16	
Silk:	Brown silk	
Tail:	Rust hackle fibres	
Body:	Stripped peacock quill	
Hackles:	Two (rust)	
Wings:	Grey duck feathers	

		Quill Gordon
Hook:	Mustad no. 94840 or 94833 nos. 12 to 20	
Silk:	Black silk or nylon	
Tail:	Blue-dun hackle fibres	
Body:	Stripped peacock quill	
Ribbing:	Very fine gold brocade	
Hackles:	Two medium blue-dun	
Wings:	Crested duck flank feather fibres	

DRY FLIES

Red Quill

Hook:	Mustad no. 94840 or 94833 nos. 12 to 14
Silk:	Black or grey silk
Tail:	Blue-dun hackle fibres
Body:	Brown stripped hackle stem
Hackles:	Two medium blue-dun
Wings:	Crested duck flank feather fibres

Royal Coachman

Hook:	Mustad no. 94840 nos. 10 to 20
Silk:	Black silk or nylon
Tail:	Golden pheasant tippet feather fibres
Body:	Front and rear sections made from peacock herl, centre in red floss silk
Hackles:	Two (dark brown)
Wings:	White duck or white goose feathers

Hendrickson

Hook:	Mustad no. 94840 or 94833 nos. 12 to 14
Silk:	Black silk
Tail:	Crested duck flank feather fibres or blue-dun hackle fibres
Body:	Back fur of red fox or musk rat
Hackles:	Blue-dun
Wings:	Crested duck flank feather fibres

See page 93.

		Adams
Hook:	Mustad no. 94840 or 94833 nos. 10 to 28	
Silk:	Black silk or nylon	
Tail:	Mixture of grizzly and brown hackle fibres	
Body:	Grey musk rat fur	
Hackles:	One brown and one grizzly	
Wings:	Grizzly hackle tips	

		Blue Dun
Hook:	Mustad no. 94840 or 94833 nos. 12 to 18	
Silk:	Black silk	
Tail:	Pale blue-dun hackle fibres	
Body:	Pale grey hare fur	
Hackles:	Pale blue-dun	
Wings:	Pale grey duck wing sections	

		Black Gnat
Hook:	Mustad no. 94840 or 94833 nos. 8 to 20	
Silk:	Black nylon	
Tail:	Hackle fibres dyed black	
Body:	Black chenille or beaver fur dyed black	
Hackles:	Two (dyed black)	
Wings:	Two grey duck feather segments	

DRY FLIES

Dark Cahill

Hook:	Mustad no. 94840 or 94833 nos. 12 to 14	
Silk:	Black silk	
Tail:	Dark brown hackle fibres	
Body:	Grey musk rat fur	
Hackles:	Two (reddish brown)	
Wings:	Crested duck or dyed mallard flank feather fibres	

Grey Fox (Flick)

Hook:	Mustad no. 94840 or 94833 nos. 12 to 16
Silk:	Primrose yellow
Tail:	Rust hackle fibres
Body:	Pale fox-cub fur or hare fur dyed pale rust
Hackles:	One pale grizzly and one pale rust
Wings:	Mallard flank fibres

Green Drake (Coffin Fly)

Hook:	Mustad no. 94840 or 94833 no. 10
Silk:	White silk
Tail:	Three elk mane hairs
Body:	White fur
Hackles:	One badger hackle and one grizzly
Wings:	Mallard flank feather fibres

Hook:	Mustad no. 94840 or 94833 nos. 12 to 16	**Light Cahill**
Silk:	Cream or pale yellow silk	
Tail:	Pale rust hackle fibres or crested duck flank feather fibres	
Body:	Pale cream red fox fur or faded racoon fur	
Hackles:	Two (pale rust)	
Wings:	Crested duck flank feather fibres	

Hook:	Mustad no. 94840 or 94833 nos. 12 to 14	**Light Hendrickson**
Silk:	Black silk or nylon	
Tail:	Crested duck flank feather fibres	
Body:	Cream red fox belly fur or faded racoon fur mixed with a pinch of pink hare hairs if the pink urine-stained belly fur of the red fox is not available	
Hackles:	Two (pale blue-dun)	
Wings:	Crested duck flank feather fibres	

Hook:	Mustad no. 94840 or 94833 nos. 10 to 12	**March Brown**
Silk:	Orange silk	
Tail:	Faded rust mink tail hairs or rust hackle fibres	
Body:	Red fox-cub fur	
Hackles:	One rust and one grizzly	
Wings:	Crested duck flank feather fibres	

139

White Wulff

See page 97.

Hook:	Mustad no. 94840 or 3906 nos. 6 to 16	
Silk:	White silk or nylon	
Tail:	Natural white hair (roebuck or calf tail)	
Body:	White mink fur	
Hackles:	Cream or badger	
Wings:	White natural hair (roebuck or calf tail)	

Ausable Wulff

Hook:	Mustad no. 94833 nos. 12 to 14
Silk:	Black silk or nylon
Tail:	Marmot hair
Body:	Light brown fox fur
Hackles:	One grizzly and one brown
Wings:	White calf tail hairs

Black Wulff

Hook:	Mustad no. 94840 or 3906 nos. 6 to 16
Silk:	Black silk or nylon
Tail:	Black roebuck or dyed calf hair
Body:	Beaver fur dyed black
Hackles:	Black
Wings:	White, made from roebuck or calf tail hairs

Blonde Wulff

Hook: Mustad no. 94840 or 3906 nos. 6 to 16
Silk: Black or primrose silk or nylon
Tail: Blonde roebuck hair
Body: Blonde fox-cub fur (or cream seal fur)
Hackles: Honey or cream colour
Wings: Blonde roebuck hair

Brown Wulff

Hook: Mustad no. 94840 or 3906 nos. 6 to 16
Silk: Brown silk or nylon
Tail: Brown roebuck or dyed calf tail hairs
Body: Brown beaver fur
Hackles: Brown
Wings: Brown or white (roebuck or calf)

Grey Wulff

Hook: Mustad no. 94840 or 3906 nos. 6 to 16
Silk: Black silk or nylon
Tail: Brown roebuck or dyed calf tail hairs
Body: Medium grey musk rat fur
Hackles: Brown and grizzly
Wings: Brown roebuck or dyed calf tail hairs

DRY FLIES

Grizzly Wulff

Hook:	Mustad no. 94840 or 3906 nos. 6 to 16
Silk:	Black silk or nylon
Tail:	Brown calf tail hairs
Body:	Yellowish fur or primrose wool
Hackles:	Grizzly
Wings:	Brown calf tail hairs

Royal Wulff

Hook:	Mustad no. 94840 or 3906 nos. 6 to 16
Silk:	Black silk or nylon
Tail:	White or natural brown tail hairs (roebuck or calf)
Body:	Front and rear portion made of bronze peacock herl, centre in red floss silk
Hackles:	Brown
Wings:	White tail hairs (roebuck or calf)

Hook:	Mustad no. 9672 nos. 6 to 10 length 3x	**The Hornburg**
Silk:	Black silk or nylon	
Body:	Flat silver tinsel, medium weight	
Hackles:	Band of grizzly and brown	
Wings:	Green hackle fibres with mallard flank feathers	
Shoulder:	Jungle cock feather	

See page 104.

Hook:	Mustad no. 9672 nos. 4 to 16 length 3x
Silk:	Black silk or nylon
Tail:	Red hackle fibres
Body:	Chenille or yellow wool
Ribbing:	Brown hackle (trim optional)
Hackles:	One brown and one grizzly
Wings:	Sections of speckled turkey feather
Head:	Black
NOTE:	Boulard original: spiral of red silk

The Joliette Hopper

See page 107.

Hook:	Mustad no. 79580 or 9672 nos. 2 to 12 length 4x
Silk:	Black nylon
Tail:	Sections of speckled turkey feather
Body:	Flat silver tinsel
Wings:	Sections of speckled turkey feather with grey squirrel tail hairs
Shoulder:	Roebuck back hairs, flared along two-thirds of the length of the hook
Head:	Roebuck or trimmed caribou hair

The Muddler

See page 111.

White Marabou Muddler

Hook:	Mustad no. 79580 nos. 1/0 to 12 length 4x
Silk:	Black nylon
Tie:	Red cement or silk
Body:	Tube of silver Mylar
Wings:	A bunch of white marabou feathers with four or five peacock tail feather fibres
Shoulder:	Natural roebuck hairs, short
Head:	Natural roebuck hair, trimmed